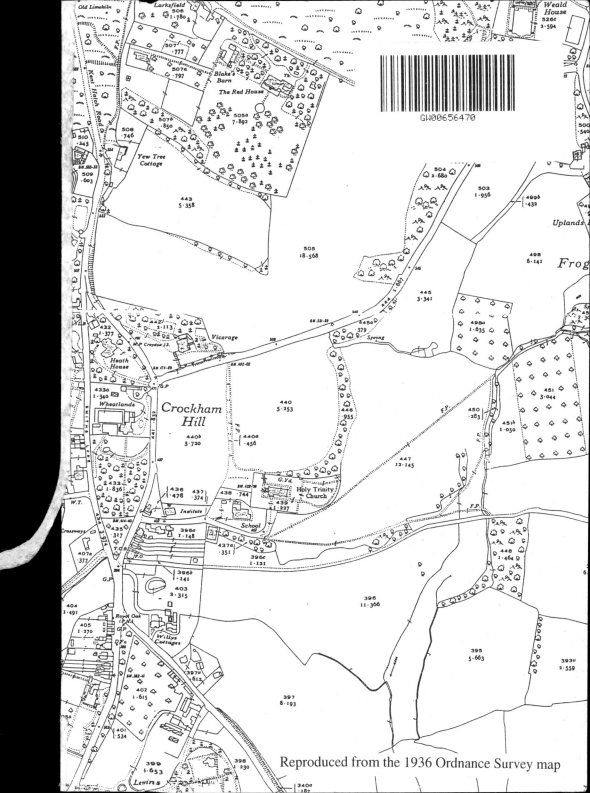

Reproduced from the 1936 Ordnance Survey map

GW00656470

A photograph taken at Pitts Cottage, Westerham during the Coronation celebrations of May 1937. From the left Mr and Mrs Paul Bankart, Jane, one of the young ladies who paid Elsie Wilson (behind her) for the privilege of being taught how to run a tea room. Next to Miss Wilson, her manageress Olive Gardner. Behind Miss Wilson is Mary Gaman. Front right is Diana ?, and second row right Sally?.

This photograph was taken in the same month that Neville Chamberlain took over from Stanley Baldwin as Prime Minister and a few days before the Duke of Windsor married his beloved Wallis Simpson. Not far away, at Chartwell, Winston Churchill, in the political wilderness, was writing his speeches which warned against the possibility of small nations falling under the power and influence of Nazi Germany and that country's persecution of the Jews. The Press began to call, with increasing force, for his return to the Cabinet but the Government still rejected his advice and individual members continued to belittle his judgement.

Westerham & Crockham Hill in the War

Researched and compiled by

Helen Long

Published by The Westerham Society
in association with
Froglets Publications of Brasted Chart

The Westerham Society

Published in 1995 to mark the 50th anniversary
of the end of the second world war

Designed and originated by
Froglets Publications Ltd, Brasted Chart,

Westerham, Kent, TN16 ILY

Tel: 01959 562972 Fax: 01959 565365

ISBN 1 872337 40 6

This book was printed and bound by
Staples Printers Rochester Ltd, Neptune Close, Medway City
Estate, Rochester, Kent ME2 4LT

By the same author:

Change Into Uniform
City of London Safari
Into France With Ease
Safe Houses are Dangerous
Greek Fire: The Massacres of Chios

INTRODUCTION

T his is not an official history. It is rather an impressionistic account of how the events of World War II appeared to the people of Westerham and Crockham Hill. The aims of the project are to show how the local people were affected by it and to describe events in Westerham and Crockham Hill within the larger history of the war.

I extend my warmest thanks to the many residents who, at my request, have searched their memories which they have shared with me with enthusiasm and often with humour.

Half a century is a long time to look back, and not everyone re-members the same events in the same way. A number of contributors have chosen to remain anonymous. I have included, in italics, previously writ-ten accounts and official records.

A list in alphabetical order of all those who contributed to this history appears at the end of the book. My thanks are due, too, to the late Arthur Yeadon, Air Raid Warden at *The Hill* during WW2 whose splendid account left for the interest and entertainment of posterity I have plun-dered as an enrichment to this book.

Readers will appreciate that memories are fallible after 50 years, and that everything in this text is taken from recorded interviews or from written accounts.

Helen Long

The Westerham Society thanks Mrs Helen Long for generously donat-ing her time and skill to convert these verbal accounts into a permanent local history. We thank her husband, Dr Aidan Long for his help in proof reading and for giving us his support for the project. We hope this book will appeal, not only to those who lived here in Westerham and Crockham Hill during those difficult days, but to everyone interested in what happened then, and how our town was turned into a war zone.

**Alan Taylor-Smith of
The Westerham Society**

Front cover illustration: *Three small children, near Valence watching George Rudd's steam-traction engine-driven threshing machine at work in September 1939. The boxes contained their gas masks. In the background is St Mary the Virgin and the churchyard. The days of peace were rapidly drawing to a close.*

CHRONOLOGY OF WW2 AS EVENTS

1938
September. Munich Conference. "No war in our time."

1939
1st September. German troops invade Poland
3rd September. Britain and France declare war on Germany
October 1939-April 1940 The 'Phoney War'.

1940
8th January. Food rationing begins in Britain
10th May. German troops invade Netherlands, Belgium,
Luxembourg and France.
Churchill becomes British Prime Minister
13th May. Dutch Queen and Government flee to London
26th May/4th June. Evacuation BEF from Dunkirk beaches
4th June. Churchill's speech *"We shall fight them..."*
10th June. Italy declares war on Britain and France.
2nd July. Hitler issues orders for Operation *Sealion* if
necessary. Invasion of Britain aim.
July - October Battle of Britain.
15th August. Battle of Britain's airfields
August. Churchill's speech *"Never in the field of
human conflict..."*
7th September. *Blitz* on London begins.
17th September. Operation *Sealion* postponed indefinitely

1941
10th - 11th May. Last major raid of London *Blitz*.
12th July. Pact of mutual assistance with USSR
7th December. Japanese attack on Pearl Harbour and war
with USA & Allies
11th December. Italy and Germany declare war on USA
& vice-versa.
18th December. Britain extends conscription
to include women.

AFFECTED THE COUNTY OF KENT

1942
1st-30th July. First Battle of El Alamein. Auchinleck halts
Rommel's advance.
8th August. Alexander appointed C-in-C Middle East.
Montgomery appointed to command 8th Army.
19th August. Disastrous Anglo-Canadian raid on Dieppe.
23rd October. Second Battle of Alamein begins.
5th November. Second Battle of El Alamein brings
Victory.
8th November. Operation Torch. Landings in Morocco and
Algeria.

1943
13th May. El Alamein campaign ends.
25th July. Mussolini overthrown and arrested
17th-18th August. RAF raid on German V1 & V2 Weapon Research
Centre at Peenemunde
13th October. Italy declares war on Germany.
4th December. Eisenhower appointed Supreme Commander
Allied Expeditionary Force (for invasion of France.)

1944
6th June. D-Day.
13th June. First V1 flying bomb raid on London.
8th September. First V2 rockets fall on London.

1945
28th April. Mussolini killed by partisans.
30th April. Hitler & Eva Braun commit suicide.
8th May. Victory in Europe. VE Day.
15th August. VJ Day.

Westerham still just at peace on Tuesday April 11th, 1939. This photograph which first appeared in The Times shows a number of ramblers on the village green before setting off on a walk of the North Downs.

Contents

1938-39: Preparing for War

IN 1939 Britain took up arms in a sober spirit having earlier embarked upon reluctant preparations for all out war.

As early as 1937, the Air Raid Warden service had been created.

By August 1938, the WVS, (Women's Voluntary Service) had come into being and Anderson shelters were being built.

In September 1938 the first barrage balloons were seen over London.

3 November 1938. Sevenoaks Rural District Council
(*SRDC*) met to discuss:

Westerham Siren: It has been recommended that the siren be moved from the Westminster Bank premises to a tower to be erected at the site of the New Fire Station at a cost of approximately £30.

28 November 1938. Westerham Parish Council (WPC) met
to discuss Air Raid Precautions and 'trenches'.

On the matter of trenches, a suggested meeting with representatives of the Sevenoaks Rural District Council. It was agreed that the Clerk reply...and that Westerham Parish Council will cooperate in the scheme...

During 1938 too, expansion of RAF Biggin Hill had taken place. After the Munich Crisis all buildings were camouflaged and a belt of trees was planted whose shadow would also help to confuse and conceal. In the autumn of 1939 the main tarmac runway was constructed, with two other runways added later. A local single-decker bus with blacked-out windows made a big detour (with an armed guard on board) so that passengers should not see what was happening at the airfield. On the way from Bromley to Westerham, passengers were picked up at the King's Arms at Leaves Green, driven round via Downe and Jail Lane and deposited back on course at the Black Horse, Biggin Hill or vice versa. Any potential spy presumably saw nothing, but the curiosity of everyone else was instantly alerted.

In January 1939 in anticipation of an outbreak of war, the decision was taken by the Woolwich Equitable Building Society to have all records duplicated and to acquire country quarters to receive evacuated members of staff and the deeds. In March 1939 Pilgrim House, Westerham, destined to become the very heart of the Society's operations, was acquired by the Woolwich Equitable Building Society for the purpose of emergency offices and a hostel. The buildings were extensively renovated, 14 dormitory huts containing in all 140 separate sleeping cubicles were then erected and additional out-buildings were built, including 12 garages, ample lavatory accommodation and a private sewage disposal unit. A strong-room with four separate entrances and exits was excavated into the chalk at 100 feet below ground level and in it was installed a Silica Gel Dehydration plant to assist storage conditions. A complete system of electrically operated fire and air-raid alarm bells was installed, tennis courts and playing fields out of doors were amongst the amenities and in 1940 a large recreation hall was added. This was the new home to which 150 members of the staff went 'for the duration'.

Alexander (Sandy) Meikle, from 1943 General Manager of the Woolwich at *Pilgrim House,* and eventually to become the Company's Chairman, settled into *Carradale* in Pilgrims' Way. Other 'Woolwich' families, amongst whom were the Sellers and the Swarbricks, as the Meikles were to do, stayed on in Westerham after the war.

Mons Bell (named after a First World War battle)
"In 1939 I called for orders on behalf of Dove the butchers, at the excavation sites of the Woolwich Equitable and in 1939 the Leeds Permanent Building Society too, on the North Downs. I was lowered in a bucket down the chalk face to ask the workmen what they wanted. Orders might be:- 'Charlie on the crane ½ lb frying steak...Bill on the pom-pom, 1lb sausages... There were several entrances. One at ground level and two more, way down. Then I had to deliver it all back to them."

9 January 1939. WPC minutes:

SRDC suggestions for the construction of trenches in the town. Voluntary labour under supervision, material to be supplied by the District Council. After some discussion...the scheme was approved. As regards voluntary labour, the Clerk to write to Major Warde asking if he would have any men available. Asked if Crockham Hill was to be included, the Clerk was requested to include this enquiry in his reply.

28 March 1939. SRDC minutes:

At a meeting of the evacuation sub-committee held at 'Inglewood', Oak Hill Road, Sevenoaks...after a full discussion it was decided to prepare a list showing:-
(1) Large houses - containing over 15 rooms.
(11) Medium houses - containing 10-15 rooms.
(111) Small houses - containing fewer than 10 rooms.
It was agreed to submit a general skeleton scheme to the Ministry of Health for the billeting of school children and teachers in large empty houses, and the request that the Minister of Health give more definite indications as to what expenses in this connection may be incurred on behalf of H.M.Government.
Hon Margaret Colville of *Packway,* Hosey Hill, Westerham was much involved with the SRDC and its plans for the evacuation from London.

17 April 1939. WPC minutes:

Grange ARP. The question of permanent ARP trenches on this site cannot be considered owing to the fact that the greater part of the land has been sold and building developments will shortly be commenced.

12 June 1939. WPC minutes:

Trenches: the SRDC submitted details of trenches proposed to be constructed on the Green. The Rev J.A. Castle proposed, the Hon. M. Colville seconded that the SRDC be advised that this Council strongly disapproves of permanent trenches being constructed on the Green.

In June 1939 the Women's Land Army came into existence when a register began to be compiled of women willing to give up their ordinary jobs for farm work if war should come.

27 June 1939. SRDC minutes:

First Aid Point, Westerham:

Plans prepared for the conversion of the Men's Club, Fullers Hill, Westerham into a First Aid Point.
Costs involved are estimated at £13.14.0.

Ambulance:

The Laundry Van purchased by Capt. Wilson has been fitted with steel carriers to take four stretchers.

"The newly-developing site at *The Grange* already had the Co-op building and the building at the far end where to-day is GA Services, but the Victoria Wine, Taylor-Smith's Antiques, the Pet shop and the dry-cleaners were not built until after the war. A brick Gas Cleansing Station with separate entrances for men and women was built prior to the war on land adjoining the Co-op but was never used and was to be demolished after the war. To-day there is a small piece of garden and a seat in its place."

Mollie Couldrey (née Parker)
"Proper ambulances were reserved for hospitals. In Westerham and other areas, for the use of WVS volunteer drivers, we were in time to be allocated vans, adapted to carry four stretchers. Ours, modified at the Sevenoaks Rural District Council's Dunbrik Depot at Sundridge, we collected from Dunton Green."

Walter (Jumbo) Gammage who had both joined the Territorials and started work at B. Horton & Sons Timber Yard in Westerham in 1929, was by 1935 Foreman at the timber yard and a Quartermaster sergeant in the Territorials:

"I was called up on 25 August 1939, a week earlier than most of the lads. All my friends who joined up as privates got 2s a day whereas I got 8s. I was out in the timber yard pushing an Austin 7 out of an old stable when the recruiting sergeant arrived, saying 'get that car going and get over to Edenbridge: you've been called up.' That was all the notice I had.

In Edenbridge I was sent flying by an approaching car which I didn't see in the blackout because it had been fitted with the new hoods on its sidelights. I landed on my head and hands. Back in Westerham with a bad headache and two huge sprained thumbs, Dr Hay came to see me in Railway Terrace: Edenbridge's first wartime casualty, two days before war was actually declared. Charlie Pulham was with my lot and so was Len Waterhouse's brother who was a cook and cooked at the King's Arms for years after the war."

Len Waterhouse
"Tiny Barnard, Charlie Pulham, the two Hobbis brothers, Victor and Alfred, Stanley Frost, 'Darkie' (Arthur) Streatfield, a number of other Territorials and I all had to report to the Drill Hall in Westerham where we picked up our rifles and from there were sent to Biggin Hill. We were billeted up there in the Royal Engineers' barracks on the edge of the airfield, South Camp, where after

the war the Westerham Press was for a time. Rumours were flying about as we paraded on the airfield, but we were soon divided up and moved around prior to some of us being sent to France with the British Expeditionary Force. Then in 1940, in the countryside behind Dunkirk we were taken prisoner and were to spend five years as POW's at Fort Rauch in Poland's Stalag XXI. On release in 1945, we marched 1,000 miles on half a loaf of bread daily to Munich where the Americans arranged transport for our return to England. N. Hoath, C. Butterworth, H. Reeves and R. Abbott remember their release."

Before the war, when Mons Bell went to Maidstone to join up, they wanted to know what he had been doing since leaving school.

"I told them I'd been a butcher for six years from the age of fourteen and that I would like to join the RASC as a butcher. So they turned me into a motor mechanic, saying it would only be for six months anyhow and when my papers came through I ended up in the Royal West Kents ...foot-slogging."

Betty Pointon (née Boniface, later Mrs Victor Hobbis)
"My husband Victor and I were married in Westerham in 1941, but as a gunner in the Royal Artillery he was taken at the fall of Singapore in February 1942 and in July, died of dysentery as a Prisoner of War in Japanese hands. Sadly he was reported missing for over a year and had not received a number of my letters, returned to me later unopened, one of which would have told him that I was expecting our child. His brother Alfred a Sgt Gunner in the RAF was shot down over Norway, leaving their parents bereft of their only two children."

Don Adams
"Tom Gorick and all of us joined in with help from the Royal Artillery stationed locally, to build an L-shaped air raid shelter at Crockham Hill's village school. We did it on that bit of green on the left as you go up towards the church, with an escape hatch at one end and an air vent. All the men in the village volunteered to help, and brought their own wheel-barrows to dig out and carry the stuff and pile it up on the top. It's still there to-day."

Throughout the weeks leading up to the declaration of war, WPC minutes record such matters as the siting of new litter baskets, the pros and cons of planting trees along roadsides, the repair of a kissing-gate and the removal at Miss Evenden's request of a telephone-box from outside her shop close to the King's Arms to a new position across the road outside the George and Dragon. (She had not approved of the illuminated goings-on inside it, visible after dark, and so unavoidably embarrassing for her customers.)

Flight Lieutenant Peter Malam Brothers (later to rise through the ranks) with his future wife Annette, and her mother Eve Wilson, in the garden of Over the Way *opposite* Pitts Cottage *in 1938. Brothers served with 32 Squadron at Biggin Hill from 1936 to August 28, 1940. He had a most distinguished war, shooting down many enemy aircraft.*

Air Commodore Peter Brothers CBE DSO DFC and Bar

"I met Annette before the war when she was working at her auntie's tea room at *Pitts Cottage*. We were married at St Mary's Church, Westerham in March 1939 and lived in a little bungalow, *Magnalvis*, at the top of Salt Box Hill, Biggin Hill. One day, when things had hotted up, she was sitting freshening her make-up with the window open and a bomb fell nearby, shattering her mirror. I decided she would be safer in Westerham and she moved into *Anne's Cottage* near the T-junction and then above Antiques owned by Auntie Elsie, and eventually to *Over the Way*, Auntie Elsie's guest house where, because of rationing, I buried in the garden about 20 gallons of aviation fuel for use in my old Bentley. As the war progressed, Annette followed me to other airfields such as Manston and we had rooms in pubs and things. Eventually when she became pregnant later in 1940 I decided it wasn't good for her to be sitting at the window counting the aircraft in and I sent her to Lancashire to stay with my mother."

When The Leeds Permanent Building Society purchased The Hill School building, known as *The Hill*, from a Mrs Ladds, Headmistress of a girls' school, they evacuated to it their entire staff from their premises in London's Regent Street. Using Welsh miners working throughout the night to dig a 60 foot tunnel into the hill behind the house and shoring it up with railway sleepers, they employed electrical contractors Drake and Gorham to lay a cable and install electricity in the tunnel which also had hurricane lamps for emergency use. The Leeds had its own fire-watchers and its ARP wardens formed part of Westerham's group of wardens.

Arthur Yeadon (known as A.Y.), the firm's London Manager and his wife rented *Rysted* in Pilgrims' Way from Mr and Mrs Rothwell, (Mr Rothwell had been a Government scientist working for the ADEE: Air Defence Experimental Establishment at Biggin Hill) who was transferred to Wales on the outbreak of war. The Yeadons were to occupy the Rothwell's house 'for the duration.' When the Rothwells returned, the Yeadons moved to live for a few years at *Ridgeway* in Trotts lane until they moved to Sevenoaks, Arthur Yeadon having at one time been Hon. Treasurer of Westerham's Men's Club. It is thanks to him that we have a detailed account of wartime activities in his part of Westerham, faithfully and at times humorously recorded for posterity."

ARP. SECTOR 50. WESTERHAM. SEPTEMBER 1939 - DECEMBER 1944.

Personnel: Sector Wardens:

E.A. Taylor. (The Mount. Member of London Stock Exchange).   C.S.Dence. (Highover. Man. Director of Brands Essence).

Wardens:

Miss Constance A. Brogden. (Secretary at the beginning of the war to Mr Brill of Solicitors Wheeler, Brill & John and later secretary to Mr Yeadon).
Mrs Ward (resigned)
Frederick G. Bailey. (Market Gardener at *Mount Lodge)*.
S. Compton Skinner. (*Plovers,* Pilgrims' Way).
Dallas L. Ralph. (Bought *Hill Lodge* in 1939. Just returned from China and lived at *Hill Lodge* with his sister Dodie).
Frank Pratt Viles (Leeds staff. Lived at *The Hill* with his wife Edith).
Arthur Yeadon (London Manager of Leeds Permanent Building Society).

On 9 August 1939, Mrs Anne Warde from *Squerryes Court,* as Village Representative for the Women's Voluntary Services for Civil Defence, advertised the urgent need of volunteers for...

BLOOD TRANSFUSION
(War Time Emergency).

Volunteers for the above are urgently needed. The Medical Research Council, under the Ministry of Health has asked the WVS if it will help to make known the need amongst their members and others, and to ask as many as possible to volunteer...It is estimated that in war time 10% of all civilian casualties will need transfusion, without which their lives would be seriously endangered...

1 September 1939, the day German troops invaded Poland, saw a trial blackout of London and the start of official evacuation though some had gone in August. Kent was, as we now know, to become the most attacked county in the country, a problem which seems not to have been anticipated by the planners who were in time, when the Germans invaded the Low Countries, to make emergency re-evacuation plans affecting many parts of Kent.

"On 3 September 1939, the first day of war, normal broadcasting was abandoned and all we got over the wireless was a load of gramophone records with Sandy Macpherson at the BBC Theatre Organ in between."

"On 3 September 1939, on a day when Britain experienced 10 hours of sunshine and the temperature climbed to 73.7 degrees, at 11.00 am the people of Westerham and Crockham Hill heard the declaration of war over their wireless sets. This was also the day on which the National Fire Service was introduced."

3 September 1939. Westerham Scout Records:

Great Britain declared war on Germany at 11 am to-day. In the evening a meeting (of the 17th Sevenoaks - Westerham Junior - Scouts Group) *was held in the club to discuss what could be done for the boys who have been evacuated from London. It was decided to run a club for any Scouts who have come down. We felt it impossible to arrange anything for everybody as the numbers are too great. The club would be open for games every evening from 6.15 to 8.45, and a subscription of 1d a week would be charged. Written permission would have to be obtained for any boy to attend.*

Neville Wells

"Laundries were subject to Ministry of Defence legislation and at Seal where we had large steam boilers, we had from the beginning, at government expense, been set up as a Gas Decontamination Centre with galvanised tanks and wire baskets. Our Westerham Laundry was also designated as essential works, with contracts for the laundry of Sevenoaks and Edenbridge hospitals, Farley Croft Evacuated Children's Home, the Angus Seamen's Home at Cudham and Caxton Home up on Limpsfield Chart. When the troops arrived in our area we also of course had to accept Army contracts for their military bundles.

My mother's mother spent the war years with us as did her unmarried sister, my great aunt, all of us living at *Uplands*. When the soldiers' bundles had been through the laundry, any socks that needed mending were brought back to us and those elderly ladies would darn them as part of their 'war effort'. Nothing would be said. It was a silent service. The socks would simply be left there and they would deal with them in the same way that they knitted string gloves for men handling steam-pipes in the Royal Navy.

My father, Stanley Wells, at the outbreak of war was visited at *Uplands* by Sergeant Wright who presented him with his Special Constable's Long-Service Medal. My father had completely forgotten that during the 1929 period of the General Strike, he had volunteered as a Special Constable and had in fact never thought to 'sign off'. He was therefore still a Special Constable when war broke out and was promptly made a Sergeant, serving in Westerham alongside a number of local Special Constable volunteers. He also continued to run the Army Cadets as he had done since the end of WWI, so that his Special Constable duties in WW2 were in fact incidental."

Gordon Edgar

"In September 1939, as soon as war was declared, our fields of standing corn were invaded by men who set up posts and wire all over them. They made pylons with scaffolding poles in the middle of a field, then took wires from them to posts they put in all along the edges of fields. This was done to stop enemy aircraft from landing. They also put a lot of old wrecked cars amongst our fields which were just ready for harvesting. They must have feared immediate invasion because despite our pleas, they just wouldn't wait until we could get the corn cut."

Westerham Women's Institute. Archives. Maidstone.

In September 1939, Westerham's WI monthly meeting, due to have taken place at Mrs Darkin's School in London Road (now Croft Hall School) *was omitted, as an outing had been arranged which was cancelled owing to the outbreak of war.*

President: Mrs Granville Streatfeild. Cottage-on-the-Hill.
Vice-Presidents: Miss Gosling. Farleyside. Farley Common.
Mrs Blackwood. Beverley. London Road.
Mrs Violet Wells. Uplands. Pilgrims' Way.
Secretary: Miss M.E.B. Morris. Darenth Towers.
Treasurer Mrs Mudd. Wychelm. Pilgrims' Way.
Press Correspondent: Mrs Eileen Duggan. Springfields.

Because Westerham was designated a 'reception area' for evacuated mothers and children, Dr Anthony Winder, living at *Breaches* when war broke out, had to wait until December 1940 before receiving his call-up papers.

"We practising doctors were asked whether we were prepared to join the forces at once. If we were, then we were advised that if ours was to be a reception area, we must not leave our practice. I therefore stayed on in Westerham until I received a directive saying that the needs of this reception area were being met and that I would now receive my call-up papers according to my age-group. I reckoned it was a somewhat off-hand and discourteous way of doing things seeing that I had volunteered for the army a year earlier."

Geoff Hoath
"Miss Coster was Post Mistress and I was Telegram Boy and was paid 1s 8d for delivering on my bike to Sundridge, 1s 3d to Brasted Chart and 6d for deliveries in Westerham. Miss Stone was Telephone Supervisor and postmen were Frederick Cull and Alfred Nicholas."

Frederick (Fred) Cull
"My father was in the sorting office in Westerham Post Office on the night before war broke out. In those days Westerham had a telegraph boy to deliver telegrams on his bike and the telephone exchange was above the post office. He was sent to deliver an urgent special packet for Mr Churchill at *Chartwell*.

At about 8.00 pm my father asked me if I'd like to cycle there with him: postal deliveries were all made on foot or by bicycle in those days and only the bulk mail was brought by van to the post office for dispersal. It was a 'railex' package which involved meeting the train at Westerham station to collect it, signing for it, taking it back to the post office for hand-stamping with the time of arrival etc. by the Post Mistress, and cycling up to *Chartwell*. But there was nobody there. The house was deserted and Mr Churchill must have hurried to London. Back we went to the post office for re-stamping and on to the station for 'railex' to get it to Mr Churchill in London.

Tom Gorick with Gordon Cox, Air Raid Warden.

Next day, September 3rd, being a Sunday, the telegraph boy was not on duty and nor was I, at Charlie Sharp's Garage. Telegrams were being received which necessitated my cycling to and from *Chartwell* about four or five times to deliver them into the butler's hand. As I cycled back up Vicarage Hill that last time I heard the siren 'go' for the first time - from Charlie Sharp's Garage - and hurried to our shelter there."

Dr Winder

"It was a Sunday morning and I'd been doing a round of visits up on Westerham Hill. As I came down the hill the siren suddenly 'went', and as it did so, two cars emerged, one from either side of Pilgrims' Way at the cross-roads, and crashed. Nobody was much hurt. None of us had ever heard the siren before so I suppose they must have been astonished and terrified and weren't concentrating. Anyhow, I claimed my statutory 12s 6d fee for attending a motor car accident."

On the day war broke out G.Pulham, ex-Royal West Kent Regiment was at Biggin Hill Airport.

I had just finished a 24-hour guard duty at the Airport's main gates and had a 24-hour pass to get my spare pair of boots studded, but before I could leave the camp I had my pass taken away from me. I later became a POW (30 April 1940 - 30 May 1945) which is a large slice of my life I will never, never forget."

Donald Downs
The Second World War came on me in slow stages. My father having somehow wangled himself on to the RAF Reserve at the age of 55, was called up in August 1939 and came home on a brief leave in uniform before going off to Uxbridge.

Newspaper headlines became daily more ominous but to me as a fifteen-year-old schoolboy it all seemed very distant. Angling by this time had become a passion in my life! The next stage of the war came on September 2nd.

I had been fishing near Four Elms and on my return in the gloaming was surprised to see a man standing in the shadows of the drive into one of the big houses as I cycled up the road to Chartwell, Sir Winston Churchill's home. He was wearing a distinctive armband that proclaimed him to be a Special Constable. It was on the 3rd - a pleasant sunny Sunday morning - that we heard the fateful wireless announcement that a state of war existed between Germany and Britain...and almost immediately afterwards we were horrified to hear for the first time the dismal wailing of an air raid siren. It was a false alarm, but initially terrifying. One of our neighbours, an elderly lady with normally immacu-

late white hair, came running up the road to us with her hair literally standing on end.

There followed hectic days making blackout curtains, putting in electric light bulbs of lower wattage, dimming car and bicycle lights, being issued with gas masks, getting used to food, clothes and petrol rationing and being issued with national identity cards. It became vital to learn the number of one's card: I can still remember mine - DJQS/106/3.

Peter Finch
"September 3rd 1939 was a good day for me. Ever since I could walk, I had had to go to piano lessons at Miss Earl's house in New Street. Then on that Sunday morning, halfway through my lesson, the siren went, our first raid warning for real. I didn't even stop to collect my music. I just hightailed it for home. Later that day my mother said I need not continue lessons any more in view of the war. Cor! What a blessing.

But my war really started well before the war, in about 1938. I was an eleven-year-old school boy at Hosey by the time it broke out. But we'd been making preparations for it well before that. We dug trenches everywhere, for what purpose I never found out, and we were all filling sand-bags. I must have filled thousands, though I never did know where they were used."

One of the first measures the local authorities undertook following the declaration of war was the evacuation from London of thousands of children. Most of them were sent into the counties closest to London, though some went further afield to the North of England and some even went overseas. The evacuation process had begun even before the formal declaration of war with mothers and babies and small children, all hung about with cardboard boxes containing their gas masks travelling to strange destinations - mostly by rail.

John Warde
"With my mother in charge, the whole of the top floor was soon filled with evacuees. All the tenant farmers, the Stevens and the Greenlees rallied round with their horses and carts to collect the children from Westerham Station and bring them to *Squerryes*. In those days we still had house-maids and God knows who else who all looked after the children.

But after about a fortnight the parents came down and started grumbling. You can imagine what my mother said. Their complaints about the children not liking the food etc. got pretty short shrift from her. She more or less told them that if they were not satisfied...result instant evacuation back to London."

"Ours came on The Flyer, having had to change at Dunton Green, of course, and many homes were awaiting them, having made all sorts of arrangements for their welcome and comfort. Sir Henry Pelham of *Currant Hill* was the local billeting officer. But for many local children the war was already an absorbing affair and a crowd of new faces around the town and at school was just another facet of hostilities."

Margaret Tulloch (née Johnson)
"My parents were allocated an evacuee called Sidney, aged about ten or eleven from the East End. He was a little horror, and a handful during the Battle of Britain. He would lie out in the garden with my tin hat on and a pair of binoculars, watching the dog-fights. And he used to race around out in the woods looking for crashed aircraft and come back with gory stories about finding airmens' flying boots with their feet still in them. He actually had two or three German airmens' vertebrae that he'd got from a crashed plane. We simply could **not** get them off him and he slept with them under his pillow every night. All those kids went rushing round on their bikes all over the place. He went back to London before the *Blitz* but not before he'd had a good caning at Hosey School from Mr Taylor who alerted my mother to the fact that he might be somewhat subdued that night - as indeed he turned out to be. But his father who was home on leave from the forces turned up in Westerham to have a row with my father who had never touched him, and warn him never to 'lay a hand on my son.' Mercifully he left us very soon after that and my parents then had a number of airmen lodging with them in this house.

I can remember seeing a big German bomber being chased by our fighters, limping back from a raid on London with one engine on fire, and seeing a little German airman out on the wing trying to put the flames out. I heard later that it had crashed somewhere to the south in the Weald area."

"Once the evacuees arrived, our school days were split into two", Olive Darby (née Hazel) remembers, as do Beryl Bellingham (née Howard) and Anne Tamplin (née Friend).
"You either went in the morning or the afternoon as there wasn't room for us all to be there at once. And when we weren't in school, we were taken for long walks or on 'outings'. We were shown over Westerham Post Office and the Brewery and we visited Harry Steven at Squerryes Home Farm to learn about milk production. Of course to-day they all do those kind of 'outings', but for us it started with the arrival of the evacuees. The only 'outings' we'd known until then were run by the Sunday Schools."

Ivory Moffatt
"We used to walk the children from St Mary's Primary School in a crocodile up to the British Restaurant for lunch, and if the siren went we all hurried down into the air raid shelter under London House in the London Road. When the evacuees arrived, we had to dodge around and share the school with them.

We really had virtually no contact with them as they brought their own teachers with them from Peckham. But shortage of space meant that many of my classes took place in Westerham Hall. We used what to-day is the 'Bar Room' at the back beside the platform which became my classroom. But we had no desks, just chairs, and the children used to kneel on the floor and put their books on the chair-seats. We also used the big main hall and in time the front room on the left as you go in as well."

Beryl Bellingham (née Howard)
"I had to leave school just before I was 14, one term earlier than I should have done as there wasn't room for us all. To spread us about, we used to be sent up from the Primary School to St Mary's Hall, taking our little rush mats with us in case there should be an air raid. When the siren went, we all had to troop down to the cellars under Miss Prentice's *London House* sweet shop, at the top of London Road."

"They were said to have arrived with the evacuees. Anyhow the school nurse used to come round checking our heads for lice. Some of us kids called her Nittie Nora the Nit Explorer."

"Before ever the war came along, lots of people had always taken in lodg-ers to help out. So I don't really think the evacuees were such a change. But most lodgers in those days were commercial travellers. They had regular stopping-off places, usually near railway stations as they travelled by train then. Some of them seemed to become permanent appendages to the house. People used to say...'you know, so and so's lodger'. And some of them stayed for years. They didn't often marry, those travelling gentlemen. Next-door had a nice man who kept his bike in the passage up the side of the house. He read gas-meters and was too old to be called up, and he was jolly good when the bombs came. Westerham was full of people staying in other people's houses for 'the duration' or until they were moved on. Then another lot would come."

John Warde
"When our evacuees left *Squerryes*, the next thing that happened was that a very officious Major arrived who told my mother that he was going to take over our house and that she would have to be gone in about two days time. Fortunately, she was very friendly with old Colonel Ponsonby who had been Colonel of the Yeomanry and as Sir Charles Ponsonby was our MP, she got straight on to him. Next time the major came round he found himself confronted by, not only our local MP, but a colonel. Anyhow, as my father was a serving officer we were allowed to live in and retain half of the house which was very important. If the army had taken it over entirely, God knows what would have

happened to it.

I can remember the hall and what is now the dining-room covered in dust-sheets with pictures and other precious things underneath them and there was a large shed in the garden which also stored furniture. I was born in 1940 and was sent off to the Heathcote-Amory's in Wales as my mother had to have a major operation after which she convalesced with her parents at their home, Roydon Hall."

Mollie Couldrey (née Parker)

"I was 28 when the war broke out and had been driving since I was 17, though no test was needed at that time, so volunteered to be an ambulance driver. A number of other girls locally also volunteered to work from the newly-formed 'Point' in Croydon Road. Under the pretty awesome supervision of Miss Maryott Whyte, head of the WVS, cousin of the then Mrs Churchill and *Nana* to Mary Churchill, we worked a rota system to man the telephone and record incidents. Sue Pelham of *Currant Hill* in Westerham, the two daughters of Major Marnham of *Chartwell Farm* and Pam Harrison of *The Red House* Crockham Hill were all quite young and hurried to join Joan Bramwell, Kitty Papillon, Mary Quirke and others at the ARP HQ. In time some of them were called up into the forces or did other war work.

Mary Churchill aged 17 must just have left the Manor House School at Limpsfield and would soon leave Chartwell for London with her parents and then join the ATS. In the meantime I took her with me on a blacked-out drive around the lanes in the vicinity of Westerham to become accustomed to the very dimmed light afforded by the newly hooded lamps, before driving an ambulance. When we got back to the ARP Headquarters in Croydon Road, an irate Miss Maryott Whyte tackled me about why I had kept Mary out so late and whether we had 'stopped off at a public house.' Perhaps she would have been even angrier if she had known that Mary, learning to drive, had also taken the wheel under my supervision. I remember a ball at the Hoskins Arms Hotel in Oxted (where else in those days?) to raise money for the war effort, to which Mary must surely have gone as did so many young local girls."

Geoff Hoath

" In those days the few post office delivery vans were parked up on the George & Dragon car park. At that time there was just a steep slope up from Post Office Square, where to-day there are stone steps, and vehicles were often started by running them down the slope."

Mary Soames (née Churchill)
During the earlier months of 1939, Winston (Churchill) was busy making

additions and improvements to a cottage at the bottom of Chartwell garden; he did a good deal of the work himself. It was intended to be a retreat for Clementine and himself in the event of war...During the first year of the war they did spend a few fleeting week-ends there, but presently Chartwell was put 'out of bounds' for security reasons...I left Chartwell to live with my parents at Admiralty House almost immediately after the outbreak of war.

Robin Fedden

The lakes at Chartwell made the place easily definable from the air by enemy planes - as a protective measure they were strewn with brushwood - and when the invasion of the Kent coast seemed imminent this was no place for a prime minister. Chartwell was closed for the war...Yet he (Churchill) could not bear separation from Chartwell. Before the war he had built himself a cottage across the garden adjoining his studio, and here he contrived rare visits, sometimes coming down briefly from London to think and relax. He came alone in 1941 to await news of General Wavell's attack on Rommel's army in the Western Desert. When he learnt of its failure he paced the park for long hours. Two years later, when he had escaped for a night to the cottage, Maisky, the Russian Ambassador, arrived on a perturbed visit.

Winston Churchill

I made one of my rare visits to Chartwell to spend the night at my cottage. The telephone announced that the Soviet Ambassador must see me at once and was on his way. Maisky arrived in unusual perturbation.

Percy Reid

His (Churchill's) only other direct reference to a wartime visit to Chartwell comes on page 774 of The Second World War Vol. IV. The Hinge of Fate. In a note dated May 27 1942, he says: "A company of Young Soldiers' Battalion of Corps. troops, Buffs were detailed for my protection when I visited Chartwell this week-end. I naturally inspected it and asked questions about its equipment..."

After detailing deficiencies of which he was told in Bren guns and Bren gun carriers and commenting that men in the Battalion had been issued with two different marks of Lee-Metford rifles, he adds:

"...Could you let me have a note on this, stating whether any other units are in a similar condition?" Having said which he touches that human note which was perhaps the greatest secret of his magnetic personality. "I request", he ends his note to the Secretary of State for War and the Chief of the Imperial General Staff, "that no trouble should be caused to the company or the battalion, as I am responsible for asking the questions, which it was the duty of those concerned to answer."

When Churchill did suddenly decide to visit Chartwell during the war, be sure it was a case of 'panic stations' for quite a lot of people. On one occasion the First Canadian Division provided the guard. A war-happy band of volunteers, they had been posted to the area as a potential nodal point at a time when the German invasion seemed imminent. They took over their duties very seriously - as Percy Cloke was to discover.

Percy managed one of Westerham's few private grocery businesses, Wood's (where to-day is Elands Veterinary Clinic.) The story goes that Fred Wood got Churchill's custom after it was suddenly discovered that in fact the firm with whom the family had been dealing in Westerham belonged to a group and was not an example of unadulterated individual enterprise. Whether the precise story is true or not it is certainly completely in character with the support which Churchill gave to the small individual trader to the end of his life.

But neither Percy Cloke nor his employer - whose name was painted in large letters on his van - meant anything to the hefty and enthusiastic Canadians who challenged Percy - a quick-witted man well able to speak up for himself - when he drove up to Chartwell with his ten hundredweight van filled with provender for the Churchill week-end.

They insisted on going through every item in his load - and repeated the practice with subsequent deliveries until Percy resorted to the device of threatening to drive back to Westerham and leave them to face the storm when it broke over an ill-provided Churchillian kitchen.

Gwenda Wood

"I joined Miss Evenden in 1938 to do the book-keeping and run her London Road china shop which in the event was to be closed down during the war with all the china and glass going up to the main shop. With only 'utility' china to sell, trade wasn't brisk. The shop in time became Westerham's British Restaurant where is now the Thai Restaurant. She told me I was to go across the road to the cellar shelter under the sweet shop at London House: that little door you can see as you come up the London Road and used to be where there was a town gaol. But I wouldn't go down there when the siren went.

We used to fire watch, about three of us at Boakes the greengrocer's in a downstairs room with a big old fire which smoked fit to kill us sometimes. We had stirrup pumps and we had to stay there till six o'clock the next morning. If there was an 'incident' we had to go out in the road and tell the right person.

We had camp beds there. We weren't supposed to go to bed, but we could lie down on them so long as one of us stayed awake. A man used to come round now and again to check that we were all there, but I don't rightly know who was really in charge of us. One night we had a whole lot of bombing up behind *Squerryes Lodge* and then there was a bomb came down behind the lodge where Peter Finch lives to-day in Quebec Square."

Westerham Scout Records.

The outbreak of war brought great changes. Most of the Rover Crew went off either to the Forces or to other war work. Gradually the older Scouts were called up for war service and only Skip Taylor and John Hooker were left to run the Troop. They kept it going through the war years, only missing a summer camp in 1940 when invasion threatened and the Battle of Britain was raging overhead.

Monday 4 September 1939. WPC minutes:

Trenches: SRDC sites of trenches for approval.
The Clerk stated that the Delagarde Farm site (to-day's Fire Station area) was the District Council's own property and the trenches were in course of construction.
Daily life in the first few weeks of World War II was hardly distinguishable from peacetime for the majority of civilians away from the front line, as the British people, on the edge of an explosive Europe, steeled themselves for the onslaught. Local authorities, expecting bombs to rain down on them within hours of the outbreak of war, had made preparations during the previous year of crisis. Trench shelters were dug, sand-bags were filled and distributed, gas-masks were issued and elephantine silver barrage balloons began floating in British skies.

"Anyone with a patch of garden was issued with an Anderson shelter, a cramped corrugated tunnel. Military conscription became law in May 1939 and the first conscripts were called up in July. In Westerham and Crockham Hill young men began to disappear and in their wake came the evacuees."

9 September 1939. SRDC minutes:

Repair of War Damage. Galvanised iron sheets, asbestos sheets, tarpaulins, timber and other materials etc. to be purchased and stored as reserve supplies for first aid repairs...The Surveyor was directed to arrange necessary supplies at an approximate cost of £500 on Housing Account for storage at Dunbrik, Sundridge.

19 September 1939. SRDC minutes:

Westerham - Fullers Hill.

...This is a narrow thoroughfare leading to the First Aid Point (Men's Club). There is space for one track only, and there is also a barrier across the

thoroughfare immediately below the entrance to the Point, preventing wheeled traffic going through. An application has been received for the barrier to be made to swing open and thus allow more freedom for ambulances. The thoroughfare was closed to vehicles so far as its lower portion is concerned by an Order of Quarter Sessions. Perhaps you will consider the application.

13 October 1939. SRDC minutes:

CIVILIAN DEATHS DUE TO WAR OPERATIONS.

The Sanitary Inspector reported as follows:

PROVISION OF TEMPORARY
MORTUARY ACCOMMODATION WESTERHAM:

In this village I have sustained considerable difficulty in obtaining places suitable for the purpose. It was suggested to me that 3 old cottages near the Old House at Home might be converted for the purpose...but the lowness of the ceilings and the very dilapidated condition of the cottages...expenditure on these buildings would not be warranted...The only alternative here is the buildings which have recently been occupied by the Phoenix Laundry Company. These are situated at the bottom of Hosey Hill near the Picture Palace...The greatest difficulty here appears to be the roof lights which would have to be blacked out.

Music and entertainment were an enormous morale booster and St Mary's Hall, Westerham proved to be a popular venue with Saturday night performances throughout the war years. Here the entertainments committee advertised their new "crazy variety programme". It was almost certainly a sell-out.

1940: The Phoney War and Dunkirk

THE 'lull' or 'Phoney War' as it came to be called, September 1939 - June 1940, with little combat despite formal continuance of hostilities, is easily forgotten. It was an anti-climax, the nation keyed up for instant horrors, fussing and fumbling and wondering what had gone wrong to produce what the French called the *drole de guerre* 'the funny war' and the Germans referred to as the *'Sitzkrieg'*, the 'sitting war'. Rationing was in full swing and things were becoming ever more difficult to buy in the shops as our merchant navy strove to keep our island supplied, harassed as it was by the enemy's aircraft and U-boats.

Then on 13 May 1940, having already over-run Belgium, the Netherlands and Luxembourg, the Germans broke through French defences to launch an offensive to trap the Allied armies. The period between the outbreak of war and the evacuation from Dunkirk in May 1940 was filled with tedium. People were obsessed by the blackout and the burden of dealing on a day-to-day basis with reluctant evacuees sometimes disruptively in their midst. Yet with no air raids hitting London and other big cities, they also shared with them their disillusionment and yearning to be back home. In the event, many were to return just in time for the *Blitz*.

Sunday 12 November 1939. Westerham Scout Records.

There was a full attendance of Scouts at the Armistice Day service at the Parish Church...There was no parade this year...we have decided to spend about £11 on a truck, mainly for the purpose of waste-paper collecting... The Scouts are collecting waste-paper with much vigour in their collecting vehicle which is a wonderful contraption with about a dozen wheels. It's in action most evenings of the week.

27 November 1939. WPC minutes:

In the course of general discussion the opinion was expressed that the Parish Council have not been allotted any duties or activities in connection with the War Services, or Air Raid Precautions. The Welfare Committee appeared to be the only part which could concern the Parish Council.

6 December 1939. SRDC minutes:

Civilian Deaths due to War Operations:

...from correspondence with the Phoenix Laundry, I understand that it is not possible to obtain the use of the necessary portion of their premises. I have therefore in company with the Surveyor, visited an old cow-shed at Delagarde Farm, close to the New Fire Station and beg to recommend that this building be converted for use as soon as possible. This building is the property of the Council.

16 December 1939. Westerham Scout Records.

The first load of waste paper was carted away.
Total weight nearly 1½ tons.

"Food rationing came in gradually, beginning with butter, sugar and bacon on Monday 8 January 1940. In March it was meat too and by July that year nearly everything in the food line was on ration. In Westerham ration books and identity cards, and the renewal of such things took place at the Employment Agency, where to-day is the Wolfe Garage. A Mr Felmingham was in charge in a simple hut alongside Sam Harding's lorry drivers' cafe."

"The first time we ever had butter was because of the coupons. Before the war we always had marg. or dripping."

"We used to get petrol for the farm tractors from Charlie Sharp's, whilst military vehicles filled up at Woolits in the High Street across the road from Sharp's Garage where to-day General Wolfe House has been built. Our farm machinery was maintained and repaired either at Charlie Sharp's or by the two Verrall blacksmith brothers and Chapman at the forge at Verrall's Corner or by Alf Nicholas opposite the Royal Standard. The Wolfe and The London Road garages did car repairs only and didn't sell petrol."

15 February 1940. SRDC minutes:

Mr Sharp of the Westerham Garage has offered the free use of a Morris 15 h.p. Tourer car for towing the Beresford Stork Pump and carrying the personnel of the Auxiliary Fire Service for the duration of the war.

21 March 1940. SRDC minutes:

Canvas Dams:

The Home Office notify the allocation of two 500 gallon dams and one 1,000 gallon dam. One 500 gallon dam has been received at Westerham and I propose that this shall be reserved for erection in an emergency at Westerham Green. Lorries to carry these dams are now being sought.

In the Spring of 1940 Germany launched her *Blitzkrieg* (Lightning war) attacks in Scandinavia and Western Europe.

9 April 1940, German troops invaded Denmark and Norway and by 10 May they were into Belgium, the Netherlands and Luxembourg. Over the next 10 days additional British fighter planes flew over Westerham on their way to reinforce Allied troops in France. But on 13 May the enemy broke through the French defences to launch a massive offensive to trap the Allied armies.

14 May 1940.

The creation of Local Defence Volunteer units was announced over the wireless by Anthony Eden. By 18 May there were armed LDV men on patrol in Kent.

On 16 May 1940 Air Chief Marshal Sir Hugh Dowding warned that sending more British fighter planes to France to try to salvage the increasingly hopeless Allied position over there could result in a total British defeat and on 18 May, Churchill reluctantly ruled that no additional fighter squadrons were to be sent to France. Then on 20 May 1940 German forces reached the French Channel coast, trapping the British Expeditionary Force. Britain was now alone against Germany.

On 24 June 1940 the County Territorial Association became responsible for their own finance and administration, records and rations. On 3 August the companies were affiliated to local infantry Regiments which meant that they could wear the Regiment's cap badge, in the case of the Sevenoaks area, the Queens Own Royal West Kent Regiment. But on 23 August, 1940 Winston Churchill was to insist that the volunteers' name be changed and that Companies be known as 'Home Guard'. In November of the same year the Battalions were numbered, Sevenoaks becoming the 20th Bn. The Royal West Kents, having 1,500 men in nine companies. And in February 1942 there was compulsory direction into the Home Guard for war work and its fully volunteer character changed until Sunday 3 September 1944 when the Home Guard units were stood down.

Westerham's Home Guard pictured early in the war. Officers in the centre of the front row
Gowell, Len Heath, Tom Webb, Bob Wood, Mr Mercer, Harry Gardiner, Fred Cull, Sid
Kimber, Mr Wood, Joe Cosgrove, Reg Austen, Tom Goodwin, Arthur Mallyon, Fre

...lude Mr Gartshore, Mr Bagnall, Mr Ralph and Hugh Farmer. Other ranks are Joe ...lliams, Harry Smith, Jim Combley, Frank Moss, Jim Mills, Eric Griffiths, Fred Smith, Mr ...ergold, Jack Isted, Harry Elliott, Mr Seal, Frank Blake, John Piggott and James Greenlees.

Don Adams

"The Home Guard in Crockham Hill was trained by the Royal West Kents. Members were Lieut Gladstone of *Lewins*, Sergeant Page (foreman at *Chartwell Farm*), Jack Friend (a cowman at *Chartwell Farm*), Mr Bishop (who worked at *Northgate* at Horn's Hill), Tom Bateman (a farmer with a small holding at Horn's Hill), Mr Chapman at *Kent Hatch Corner*, Mr Drake (a gardener at *Larkfield*), Mr Hewitt, (a gardener at *The Red House*), Mr Roberts (a gardener at *Rusholme*), my father (a gardener at *West House,* Ernie and Ron Wilmer (both farm workers at *Hurst Farm,* Percy Hedges (a farm-labourer at *Chartwell Farm*), Mr Fowler (who lived in retirement opposite *Lewins*, two farm workers (who lived down at *Capeham Farm)* and myself, Don Adams (a farm worker from Deanery Road Crockham Hill but working at *Squerryes Home Farm* in Westerham).

We grew flax at *Squerryes* and we were asked by the government to experiment with sunflowers too, and of course lots of farmers grew sugar-beet to help out with the sugar ration. I ploughed up Wolfe Park which had never been ploughed before. We used an International Track Tractor, a TD6 to do it as that first ploughing was heavy going. Even the front of *Squerryes Court* was all ploughed up and planted with oats all around the lake."

Bob Wood

"At *Force Green Farm* when the Canadians and Americans came over, we were asked to cater for them by growing sweet-corn. It did very well in the field alongside *Courtlands* in the London Road and so did what we called catch-crops, parsnips and carrots and suchlike in that nice easy sandy soil. We carried on with the dairy herd and we kept lots of chickens. Most things needed on the farm were in short supply and form-filling was endless and essential for fertiliser which was only allocated if a real deficiency could be proved, for tractor and other tyres and for the hiring of machinery from the Kent War Agricultural Executive Committee."

Peter Shypitka (Mr Peters to the many who knew him in Westerham at Cullen's at the top of the London Road.)

"I came across with the First Canadian Corps troops in 1940, married my English wife Elsie in 1942 and, back from Europe after VE Day, returned home to be demobilized. We came back from Canada in 1949 and in 1952 when Cullens bought Ryders out, I became manager for the next 35 years. Bacon, fats, sugar and one or two other things were still on ration at that time, and I remember the so-called 'sweet corn' that was grown specially for us in the UK during the war years. It was most kind and thoughtful of them to do so, but we would have called those small kernels 'maize' which in Canada we would have fed to our animals!"

Phil and Ernie Fleet

"There were contract thrashing gangs with casual workers who travelled around. George Rudd operated a steam traction engine and Arthur Mallion had a mobile tractor and used to come to *Force Green Farm*. Between them they covered the whole of this area."

"I saw a cow with an incendiary bomb driven right down into its back. We used to go round ploughing up for different people because Jack Steven of this farm was on the Kent War Agricultural Executive Committee. He and Jim Greenlees and William Alexander used to go round telling different farmers what they'd got to plough up. Course, lots of them didn't have the implements. So one or other of them would say 'OK, we'll send someone along to do that for you'. As many dairy and stock farms simply were not equipped for ploughing up grassland and the drilling and harvesting of corn, the necessary equipment had to be hired or another farmer contracted to do the work at charges fixed by the KWAEC."

"I was driving the caterpillar tractor at the time so I used to have to go as far afield as *Guildables* the other side of Crockham Hill. And one night before I went to work, there was a raid just close to Edenbridge with a lot of incendiaries dropped on a farm down there. The vet, Mr Bruford from Sevenoaks happened to be there at the time and was taking an incendiary out of the back of this cow. I would imagine the government would've compensated the farmer for the loss of that animal. Bombs fell all around *Force Green Farm*. You didn't have to dial 999 or contact anyone. There was a raid on and all the right people were already watching and listening and taking action over any incident."

Bob Wood

"From *Force Green Farm* we did two nights Home Guard a week: one at Edenbridge and one at Westerham. Our Headquarters was at *Winterton House* with Major Bagnall of *Farley Grange* in command and Freddie Swarbrick who was evacuated to Westerham with the Woolwich Equitable Society, and who was to stay on after the war, as second in command. (Retired) General Currie was a 'private' with us and there was Hugh Farmer from *Churchgate* and who was in a 'reserved occupation' at the House of Commons, and Capt. Douglas Evison from the Wolfe Garage, and we used to drill behind the old Grasshopper on the Green. When we first started off we had broomsticks and we had to take our own blankets and go down to *Charman's Farm* to patrol the railway line along there. Then we got bits and pieces of uniform and arms and by that time the Woolwich at *Pilgrim House*, which had been a boys' preparatory school run by people called Hamilton, had the first Home Guard platoon up there, and being as we were close to them, we had to report up there for training."

26 May - 4 June 1940.

"It was the busiest week Southern Railway had ever known. More than 250,000 men brought into Dover and Folkestone from Dunkirk to travel to Tonbridge and beyond. At Edenbridge they threw letters out of the train windows on to the platform, knowing that the railway staff would post them. Their families would at least hear that so far, they were safe and home from France. They were coated and shiny in black oil to which sand still clung and like zombies they lay slumped, piled upon each other in carriages and corridors. As the trains pulled up, the strong were helping the weak and wounded, tears of exhaustion on unshaven faces as they reached for the cups of tea being urged upon them by willing hands."

Don Adams

"I had my first experience of what was going on, because all the lads were coming back from Dunkirk in the troop trains, all shot to pieces with blood and sand on them. They were pulled up alongside the coal trucks at Edenbridge Top Station on Marlpit Hill. The WVS ladies were giving them buns and suchlike and cups of tea. But some couldn't even be bothered to get to them, and we kept offering them lighted cigarettes through the train windows. One took the whole packet when I handed it to him: but that was alright. They were all in, and lots of them were fast asleep all over their mates."

Joy Lee (née Sutherland)

"Lorry loads of troops drove through Westerham, full of tired, dishevelled and disillusioned men. Everyone along their route came out with cups of tea etc. I can remember buying up Mr Hollingworth's entire stock of (very scarce) oranges and throwing them into the trucks as they passed."

Freda McBride (née Wright)

"I was working at *Pilgrim House* as an office girl, doing accounts and cycling to and from Crockham Hill. A German aircraft was brought down behind *Pilgrim House*. All the crew were killed."

Bob Wood

"Some horrible little boys came up and scrounged bits and pieces. There were always some with their bikes like vultures. They kept their eyes and ears' open and were quick to visit any crashed plane and see what pickings there might be. At school you could show off your war trophies. I suppose it didn't really matter that much. They were dead Germans after all, and they were doing dreadful bombing of our people. Kids weren't exactly having it good in those days. No sweets, no fireworks, their Dads away at the war and suchlike. But they must have seen some pretty grisly things which their parents didn't get told about, or they would have forbidden them."

"Bernard Johnson was Superintendent of the St John's Ambulance Brigade based in the barn adjacent to *Winterton House* where to-day live the Hilton family, and there was a First Aid Point manned by the Red Cross at the Men's Club in Fullers Hill where children were innoculated and casualties were treated."

Bert Thorneycroft
"At the Men's Club you could have a hot bath on Friday nights, but you had to book up and take your own towel and soap along with you. It was run by a committee with Bert Philips, a postman, in charge and there was a huge boiler for heating the water."

"Major Bagnall of *Farley Grange* was C.O. of Westerham's Home Guard. Sir John Dean who was knighted for his work during the war on trans-Atlantic cables and *PLUTO* (Pipeline Under the Ocean) lived at *Moreton House*. And Gerald Williams, later of *Crockham Street*, Crockham Hill (now *Crockham House*) was credited with the acronym *PLUTO*. *Farlowe* became a military base with tanks and military vehicles parked in serried ranks under khaki scrim netting all over the Common."

Phil Johnson
"My sister did some tracing for *PLUTO*, very early in the 1940s when she was with Johnson & Philips. Usually when the tracings had been used for blueprints they were scrapped: but I still have copies. My sister used to bring them home to reclaim the linen by boiling and make clothes from them. In fact some of the tracings that became underwear were probably TOP SECRET long before they were worn!"

31 May 1940. SRDC minutes:

Westerham First Aid Point:

Dr Roffey (Bessels Green) reported that further equipment was required by Dr Hay for this Point. The Committee directed Dr Roffey to endeavour to obtain a stock of the required equipment to be kept by the Westerham branch of Boots the Chemists so that it might be purchased in case of emergency.

Following the collapse of France and the Dunkirk Evacuation in May/

June 1940, invasion from across the Channel was a very real threat. Of Britain's anti-invasion preparations the one that most inconvenienced the ordinary civilian was the order (31 May 1940), for the taking down of, or painting out of...

'...any sign which furnishes any indication of the name of...or the direction of...or the distance to any place.'

The removal of signposts was followed by a wholesale uprooting of milestones, the defacing of the names of towns on war memorials and the painting over of shop and other signs identifying the town or village. Bus destination signs were amended to 'The King's Arms', or 'Top of the Hill'. Railway station names marked out with whitened stones, were removed. Telephone boxes and directories, newsagents' advertisement boards, Mothers' Union banners, parish magazines in churches and bus timetables were always liable to be offenders. England had become a mystery place in which you had to find clues, guess where you were. A wartime photograph taken in a car park in Oxted shows a gathering of uprooted signposts with local names on them, all hidden away.

"Some of us offered baths to the 'barra boys' with cups of tea to follow, cooked their food for them and helped with their washing and mending. But in certain situations there might be a kind of depot or cook-house catering for a group of balloon crews close by."

Bob Wood
"There was one of those just a few yards behind our *Force Green Farm* cottage. They were no trouble and life went on just as usual, except that we had Land Army girls to help out and there were also in due course Italian and German prisoners of war with POW arm-bands. Nobody seemed to be in charge of them and they were brought over from a camp at Tonbridge or at Tandridge."

Arthur Yeadon
A German bomber crashed on the hillside North of Pilgrim House. I can remember it was a Sunday night and I was awakened from my sleep at The Hill where I was serving as an Air Raid Warden by a terrific roar. The curtains were drawn back and a plane went past my window obviously in a dive which was to be its last.

Before I could get to the window. I heard a crash...and before I could get downstairs Skinner had phoned with the approximate location of the incident. I met him along the road and off we went. It was pitch dark and it was no joke scrambling over that hillside through barbed wire fences and tripping up in rabbit holes. We had picked Bailey (from Mount Lodge, Westerham Hill and also an ARP Warden) up along the way. Apparently he knew the country better than

Skinner and I because he was there long before us. What a mess it was, the plane was half buried in the hillside and what was visible was blazing. I had often read of the acrid smell of burning flesh, but until then had never experienced it. It was hours before I got the smell out of my nose. With what I had smelt and what I had seen, my breakfast did not appeal to me the next morning. I think it was later ascertained that there had been a crew of at least four men in the plane.

"Prior to the Battle of Britain, Hosey School boys were put to work for the war effort. We opened up some virgin land at Hosey for vegetable plots in the 'Dig for Victory' campaign, to supply the school canteen. This I enjoyed better than arithmetic any day. We also collected sackfuls of acorns for pig feed."

"As a school-boy, I spent hours up by the Fire Station. Things were always happening there and they had a canvas emergency water-tank thing we used to swim in till they sent us packing. We used to climb up outside the Fire Station and look in through the window of the mortuary which was adjacent to the Fire Station. They used to leave the window open for ventilation I suppose, and a number of our pilots and several Polish and German airmen too were brought in there.

In that hot summer of 1940 the buzz would go around that there was a corpse in there and we used to go along and stand on a stone to peer in through the window. Bodies were laid out on the slab and I can remember that their faces, eye-lids and curled back lips were all burned black. The smell was the same as you got at the site of a crash. There weren't so many Germans as there were Allied airmen. Yes, distinctive aromas of those war years for me were of those crashes where there lingered on the unforgettable smells of hot oil, hot metal and burned flesh."

Ethel 'Diamond' Charman (née Allen)
"My husband had been brick-laying for Durtnell's at Biggin Hill aerodrome, but in time the work came to an end and there was practically no building going on then. So around 1940 when the bombing started, he became a full-time fireman. I also worked in the Croydon Road, as a fire-woman. If nothing was happening it was very boring and at night it could be bitterly cold when the electric fire died on you and your opposite number was asleep until it was her turn to take over from you. Jessie Holman worked there too: she used to play the accordion and her husband drove for Liptons. My husband as a fireman was required to take part in one of the post-mortems. He found it very distressing. The only time that I had any contact with the mortuary at the HQ was an incident where a child had been found dead under somewhat suspicious circumstances.

But as the war was on, I think they said it had died of natural causes. It was quite a large baby which had probably been the child of an affair with one of the many troops stationed locally, and it appeared to have been strangled.

10 June 1940. WPC minutes:

German Gun: the Chairman stated that he had received *a letter from the Territorial Army and Air Force Association of the County of Kent. In view of the urgent need for obtaining metal of all kinds, the Association feel that it would be in the best interests of the county at the present time to dispose of this gun.* (It stood on Westerham Green.) *A later letter stated that the Secretary has written to the appropriate military authority asking them to issue the necessary instructions for its disposal.*

Joan Thorneycroft (née Lelliott)
"We youngsters used to say, 'I'll meet you by the gun...sometimes adding...when the band plays...that was Westerham's Town Band which before the war used to perform outside the George and Dragon on Saturday evenings, conducted by Mr Bennett who ran a newsagent/tobacconist's business in the town."

June 1940. Government leaflet:

IF THE INVADER COMES:

DO NOT GIVE ANY GERMAN ANYTHING. DO NOT TELL HIM ANYTHING. HIDE YOUR FOOD AND YOUR BI-CYCLES. HIDE YOUR MAPS. SEE THAT THE ENEMY GETS NO PETROL...THINK ALWAYS OF YOUR COUNTRY BEFORE YOU THINK OF YOURSELF.

**IMMOBILISATION OF VEHICLES
IN THE EVENT OF INVASION.**

PETROL VEHICLES: REMOVE DISTRIBUTOR HEAD AND LEADS AND EMPTY THE TANK OR CARBURETTOR. DIESEL-ENGINED VEHICLES: REMOVE THE INJECTION PUMP AND CONNECTION.

HIDE THE PARTS REMOVED WELL AWAY
FROM THE VEHICLE.

---

17 June 1940. SRDC minutes:

Westerham Siren:
...that the present operator had been forced to resign his post as a result of illness. The Committee directed that a letter of thanks be sent to Mr W.C.Sharp, the Siren operator, for his past services, and instructed the Surveyor to arrange for the Siren to be operated from the Wardens Post. (At the New Fire Station).

28 June 1940. SRDC minutes:

Old Fire Station, Westerham:
...that it had been suggested that the Old Fire Station, Westerham could be converted into an air raid shelter.

Westerham Siren:

...that as the Westerham Siren was now controlled from the Warden's Post, an 'Elsan' Closet would be necessary, the estimated cost being £4.10.0.

9 July 1940. SRDC minutes:

Deterrents against enemy landings. (CONFIDENTIAL).
...the Council is forthwith to obstruct obvious potential landing grounds and as a matter of urgency, although outside the scope of Air Raid Precautions, the Committee directed the Surveyor forthwith to:-

(a) arrange for a survey of the district to ascertain such grounds;
(b) commence the thinning of trees at Hanging Bank etc. and the use thereof as obstructions;
(c) compile a list of volunteers, for use;
(d) take such other steps as may be necessary and charge the costs to Highways Account and recover same from H.M. Government.

The Committee desire to bring to the attention of the Council matters which are arising necessitating urgent action, and which are not within the scope of the air raid precautions but are in some cases closely allied thereto. Such matters include the above, also Repair of War Damaged Property and Civilian Deaths due to War Operations. The Council are recommended to authorise this Committee to act in connection with these matters.

10 July 1940 saw the beginning of The Battle of Britain which was to end on 17 September when Hitler postponed officially his planned invasion of Britain 'until further notice.' During the first phase, lasting until 12 August, the *Luftwaffe* attacked British convoys in the English Channel and English south coast ports to lure British fighters into combat against much larger formations of German aircraft based at newly captured French airfields.

16 July 1940. Hitler ordered preparations for operation *Sea Lion* to be made for an invasion of Britain to take place 'if necessary.'

19 July 1940. Hitler issued 'a plea for peace' to the British to enable Germany to consolidate her conquests.

22 July 1940. The British Government rejected the German peace bid.

29 July 1940. WPC minutes:

The Gun: Ministry of Supply: The Gun is to be dealt with under a large clearance scheme of war trophies which is now in hand. The Clerk also reported on conversations he had had with the Ministry, and strong comments on the delay in removing it were made, especially in view of the wireless appeal.

Scrap Metal: At various times enquiries were made regarding the collection of scrap metal and it was to be stated that the present arrangements are in the hands of the Sevenoaks Rural District Council...it was maintained that the Parish Council could be useful, particularly with regard to the collection of scrap metal, billeting arrangements and arrangements for refugees.

Wartime activities of WPC:

Cr G. Streatfeild asked if the Parish Council has been and is being ignored in all war matters. The Chairman said they were all in the hands of the District Council. Cr Streatfeild maintained the Parish Council could be very useful, particularly with regard to the collection of scrap metal, billeting and arrangements for evacuees, and he felt the Parish Council should be given every opportunity.

Mollie Couldrey (née Parker)

"My sister-in-law had given me a splendid complete set of saucepans and fish-kettle as a wedding present, which for lack of much space in our *Farley Cottage* I had put on the window-ledge which overlooked Farley Lane. People used to admire them until one day somebody came banging on the door saying something about saucepans and the scrap-metal collection. Anyhow, I promptly removed them from sight, determined to hang on to them, and felt a bit guilty and unpatriotic, even though I did hand in other saucepans that I had in reserve."

Viola Therese Beville, aged 45, died on 16 August 1940 during one of Hitler's major assaults on south-east England. On that day more than 300 high explosives were dropped, killing 116 civilians. The Luftwaffe's targets were the airfields and Biggin Hill which had already been badly mauled had been singled out in the morning for an attack of unbated fury. Despite the heavy bombing it was another great day for the RAF; enemy aircraft destroyed was 72 against 22 Spitfires and Hurricanes.

Viola's funeral took place at St. Mary's Church and the parish register indicates that the family were not charged for the services of choir, organist, vicar or clerk — a gesture that was appreciated by the large congregation.

Some years later this entry appeared in the church visitors' book:

Peaceful, lovely church. I was here as a soldier in 1940 when Farley Common was bombed with one fatality, the wife of the ARP warden. I went to the morning Service the Sunday after when it was announced from the pulpit as Westerham's first war casualty. — Arthur Spore, Ipswich

1 August 1940. Hitler ordered acceleration of invasion plans.

13 August 1940. Phase Two of the Battle of Britain. German attacks were now directed mainly at British airfields near the coast, radar installations and aircraft factories. Despite a favourable kill-loss ratio during this period, losses became an anxious concern for the British and Westerham was in the thick of all the comings and goings.

16 August 1940. "A stick of bombs fell, spanning Toys Hill and Verrall's Corner. The last bomb of the stick crashed on Farley Common where it landed beside a car, killing the driver Viola Therese Beville, (nicknamed 'Birdie'), daughter of Dr Russell of *Winterton House*, and her two dogs. Her own home, *Windmill Field* where Mollie Cosgrove lives today, was just close by. When a first aid team reached her, she appeared to be uninjured, still sitting at the wheel of her car. But she was said to have died after all the air had been expelled from her lungs by the close proximity of the bomb's explosion. Another bomb of that stick crashed in the middle of the A25 just outside John Hooker's house, number 91, demolishing a row of *Brewery Cottages* next to George English's cafe. Those cottages were never rebuilt and there's a small strip of public garden there now with a seat".

20 August 1940. An emergency meeting of the Parish Council was held at The Library, The Green, Westerham was held to consider the provision of a public Air Raid Shelter on, or near to the Green, in addition to those at Delagarde Farm and Costells Meadow. The basement of the old Cooperative Society's premises on the Green was inspected and found suitable with estimated accommodation for about 100 persons.
It was agreed that a very strong and urgent letter be sent to the Emergency Committee of the Sevenoaks Rural District Council, asking them to take immediate steps to make such provision. The question of shelters for the school children was raised. The Reverend J.A. Castle promised to discuss the matter with the School Managers with a view to bringing pressure on the authorities.

24 August 1940. Phase Three of the Battle of Britain saw Germany intensifying her efforts to destroy Fighter Command with massive and repeated raids on key airfields such as Biggin Hill and on industrial targets. Night attacks were stepped up and the RAF shortage of pilots became critical.

25 August 1940. Berlin was bombed by the RAF in retaliation for the accidental bombing of London the previous night.

The third bombing of Biggin Hill was carried out (not by Dorniers but) *by nine Junkers 88s which had followed the Ashford-Reigate railway line at low level before swinging north to take "The Bump" (as it was affectionately called) by complete surprise. The damage caused was appalling.*

The cookhouse, workshops and the NAAFI were destroyed. Airmen's barracks, the sergeants mess and the Waafery were made uninhabitable. One hangar was blown up, two aircraft destroyed and most of the station's transport was set on fire. Worst of all an air-raid shelter crammed with airmen received a direct hit and was reduced to a yawning crater full of rubble and mangled bodies. The death toll was 39.

In the airwomen's trench where steel-helmeted WAAFs were packed together, an explosion blew out the entrance and in another blast the concrete walls caved in. Those inside were buried under stones and earth. The girls, protected by their helmets lay in a heap together, waiting to be dug out.

After the first bomb the electric lighting failed and the emergency battery set was used. This faded after the third bomb. Gas and water supplies were also cut off. Villagers in Biggin Hill who had seen the Junkers approaching, following the Westerham Road ran to the airfield as the all-clear sounded.

The entombed WAAFs, under tons of earth, were brought out one by one, the rescuers tearing frantically at the earth with their hands. Most of them were safe but dazed and shocked. One was dead — Corporal Lena Button, a nursing orderly from Tasmania.

The women were taken to the sick quarters and, as night fell, work began on the crater that was the airmen's shelter. By the light of vehicle headlights trained on the rubble the bodies were carried out one by one. Eventually a team of miners was brought in but there was no hope for those inside.

Some of the bombs that fell at Biggin Hill on 30 August 1940

"I was told that there were Dorniers zooming around up there (Biggin Hill) and that the people manning the primitive radar thought they were Blenheims. They were similar in shape, Dorniers and Blenheims, and as the fighter planes were coming in to refuel, the Dorniers just followed them in. It was said that that disastrous raid on Biggin Hill was the result of inexperienced personnel confusing them and therefore not taking appropriate action. Several of those girls were killed. I saw them digging out where they were, and some who survived were modestly pulling their little Air Force blue skirts down as they were dragged clear from under the rubble."

Margot Clark (née Sumner)
"I was living with my parents in Bromley whilst my husband of just a few days was a prisoner of war. I was driving a great pantechnicon of a YMCA mobile canteen full of everything the troops could need (from a pin to an anchor, they used to say,) when we were sent for, to go up to Biggin Hill. It was the morning after the devastating raid on the air station.

While we were parked there, feeling more welcome than ever at this time of emergency, a 'Red Warning' was received announcing enemy bombers approaching our coast yet again. We saw the instant response as those very young airmen (who looked to us to be just 18 or so years old) were scrambled. Climbing into their planes lined up on the large tarmac area behind the buildings we see from the main road today, instantly they were gone. As they disappeared into the distance we held our breath and prayed they might all return safely.....which we actually saw them do. Emerging from the air raid shelter, we watched as they rolled their small aircraft over and over: clearly they had seen off the intruders."

6 September 1940. SRDC minutes:

Deterrents on Landing Grounds:
...that this work has now been completed but that other fields might be required to be done. The approximate area covered is 1800 acres.

WI Crockham Hill. (WI Archives Maidstone).

2,875 lbs plum jam made in the summer of 1940. Special Government allowance of sugar so that a bountiful crop of fruit should not be wasted.

7 September 1940. Phase Four of the Battle of Britain began. To retaliate for the bombing of Berlin, the Germans shifted their concentrated attacks from British fighter airfields to London. Civilian casualties were heavy and much damage was done, but the reprieve for Biggin Hill enabled it to recover and to prepare to meet the onslaught as huge raids were directed against London.

Freda McBride (née Wright)

"At the Woolwich they called it 'the grid', because it was all done on squares, that storage place they dug out of the North Downs behind *Pilgrim House*. All the Woolwich records were on the sides of the cubes. They were duplicate records, not the day's accounts or anything like that. Duplicate records taken every quarter, which showed the balance of accounts. That was all it showed, and it had to be kept up-to-date. The Head Office was evacuated and all accounts of the Society were concentrated there."

Edna Peake

"The staff lived there and went home at the week-ends even when the *Blitz* was on they went home, and came back shattered. A lot of them lived at Eltham and Woolwich all along the river front. Tate & Lyle's Silvertown sugar refinery was a shattering experience. Those who came back from there would to-day be said to have been 'in a state of shock and in need of counselling', though nobody talked about that sort of thing in those days. The Woolwich laid on a coach for them to go to and from London at the week-ends."

12 September 1940. SRDC minutes:

The Paddock, Westerham:

The Clerk presented 3 tenders for the erection of a Communal Shelter at The Paddock, Westerham, for the 5 wooden Council bungalows, to accommodate 25 persons, and the lowest of these, that of Messrs. R. Durtnell & Sons Ltd., in the sum of £75 be accepted.

15 September 1940. Huge bomber raids on London were driven off by the RAF with very heavy losses to the *Luftwaffe* on what was later to be known as 'Battle of Britain Day.'

30 September 1940. Hosey School Records.

Considerable air fighting could be heard overhead and bombs were dropped. The boys took shelter under their desks.

"Mum shamed us by making us wear our shirt-tails hanging out at the back so's we'd show up as we went up and down Hosey. At the beginning of the blackout there were more casualties from cars and people bumping into things and each other than from enemy action. You were everlasting saying 'sorry' to a lamp-post or a pillar-box."

"A number of fighters came down just short of Biggin Hill, along the Pilgrims' Way, gliding in and crash-landing in Hundred-Acre, that large area between Westerham Hill and Hog-Trough Hill, despite the fact that posts had been put in all over that field in the early part of the war to stop German gliders from landing there should they attempt an invasion. At that time there were posts set in all over the place in any open area where a landing might be attempted."

Arthur Yeadon

On the night of 9 October 1940 our system of (ARP) watches justified itself in so far that we were able to report an incident in Westerham itself of which the Wardens at Main Post knew nothing. Bailey and I were watching it at my home and at about half past three in the morning we heard a stick of bombs come down, and saw flashes in what appeared to us to be in the direction of Squerryes. There was a hectic barrage going on at the time and when we reported to Main Post they had heard nothing. Actually, it was one of the biggest incidents in the district - Sharps Garage was damaged and houses in the High Street, some of which had to be demolished later. I think it was at this incident that Warden Hoath distinguished himself.

The raids slackened off a bit after Christmas 1940 and we were able to get some sleep in a real bed. It was not until April and May of 1941 that we had anything hot. Perhaps the worst raid of the war so far as London was concerned was on May 10th 1941, and in this raid Westerham had its luckiest escape when 19 high explosive bombs were dropped across the Paddock and not one exploded. There was some slight damage and minor injuries, but one shudders to think what might have happened had they all gone off - Westerham would have been blown to bits.

Then we had a very long lull from June 1941 to January 1944, and to use an army expression, we began to get somewhat 'browned off', as Air Raid Wardens. Then Jerry started with his second fire blitz...The hills on the other side of Westerham seemed to have the bulk of the incendiary bombs and we on Pilgrims' Way had a grandstand view. I remember very well one night standing in my garden watching the incendiary fires in the woods, and at the time there was a terrific barrage from the London guns. Then suddenly a nightingale tuned in as though it were the most peaceful Summer night and did not seem to be at all worried by the inferno going on around.

TROOPS ONLY

LONDON IRISH RIFLES

Present

'Shamrock Pie'

VARIETY AT ITS BEST

AT

S. Mary's Hall

ON

WEDNESDAY NEXT

December 4th

at 7.30 p.m.

Admission 3d.   Pay at the door

NUMBERS LIMITED

HOOKER BROS., PRINTERS.

Two of the veterans who helped to form Britain's great amateur army. These men had a vital task — they were guarding the gates to Chartwell.

1940-41: Fear of invasion

T he Canadians were all over Crockham Hill Common, spread right the way across the Chart to *The Salt Box* and all through the woods there on Limpsfield Chart and Crockham Hill and Hosey and around *The Warren*. Their vehicles covered with scrim netting were dispersed under the trees and the men had dug slit trenches all over those commons. Some are still there if you look for them."

Phyllis Hayden (née Gibbs)
"My father was for many years butler at *Trevereux Manor* where I grew up. During the war I nursed at the Limpsfield Chart Henry Radcliffe Convalescent Home for Merchant Seamen (now Marie Curie Cancer Research).

The Canadians were always getting drunk and firing off their revolvers and the girls went wild about them. The men were there long enough to form relationships with a number of local girls who must have known that they were here to-day but would be gone to-morrow. Some of them were married women whose husbands were away at the war and some became pregnant. There were Canadian officers at *Cronklands,* French Canadians at *Tenchleys Park* and it was said at the time that someone was signalling from up Woldingham way. The Germans must have been trying for the arms dump at Staffhurst Wood and it was a miracle that though masses of bombs fell on the Chart, none actually landed on all that ammunition. I believe that in time they caught up with whoever was signalling to enemy planes."

"Those French Canadians helped themselves to apples from our trees and even dug up the onions in our gardens and allotments. We would have liked to make them feel welcome but they seemed to threaten us by their sheer numbers and their behaviour."

Don Adams
"Up the loop road in Crockham Hill, what they now call Smith's Lane though it never was then, along there, were the 176 battery of heavy artillery. All the big guns under the trees and out of sight, from level with the post office right up to the top by *Cobblers* - about ten or twelve big guns tucked in there. That lot was English and THEY were waiting to go to France too. In the Goodley Stock road, from the first bend above *Squerryes Farm* right up to the top of Goodley Stock, was one long line of what I think were Sherman tanks - all parked close in

Evacuated children of an LCC nursery school found new and interesting things in Froghole Lane at Crockham Hill. There was a nursery at Little Mariners and Rusholme was full of children.

against the rhododendrons on the edge of the road under the row of oak trees up there, hidden from the air."

Donald Parker
"*Rusholme* was full of children evacuated by the LCC, and we understand that Joachim von Ribbentrop was a visitor to the house before the war, when he was German Ambassador in residence at the German Embassy in Carlton Gardens. It was in those days, as a London socialite that he was reckoned to have been a guest of the then owners, the German Melchers family."

Sally Cobley (née Robertshaw)
"At *Heath House*, Crockham Hill, commandeered for the Canadian Army, to-day's lawn was where they parked their military vehicles, and when excavating for a swimming pool years later, the chosen site was found to have been their war-time 'can' dump."

Anne Tamplin (née Friend)
"We used to scrounge the odd penny from the soldiers around Crockham Hill to buy sweets. They had a NAAFI van that used to come round to the troops and they could buy sweets, chocolates, razor blades and suchlike, so we kids used to get sweets from them without coupons."

A highly disagreeable task undertaken almost everywhere around the country was making camouflage nets, much in evidence at this time on Commons all around Westerham. Net-making frames were set up in village halls and even in large private houses. In some cases dedicated 'net-making' women would drop in whenever they had a few hours to spare. Volunteers knotted strips of rag on to the nets, the dye leaving their hands and clothes deeply stained. Crawling about with bruised knees and aching backs, elderly women drove themselves on for that extra hour which meant so many square feet of cover for the British army. Members of the WVS who regularly 'went netting', remember it as the filthiest job they had ever undertaken. In Westerham Joan Bramwell spent hours at this most important work, upstairs above where to-day is GA Property Services on the corner of the row of shops, opposite *Winterton House.*

"That camouflage factory was run by the WVS and they always seemed to be tall, horsey-faced old toffs. I remember they had a sign up in the window that said: THEY ALSO SERVE WHO ONLY STAND AND CAMOUFLAGE. I think they just knotted strips of khaki and green hessian on to the nets." At that time only the Co-op. building and the one at the other end existed, with a space in the middle and a purpose-built brick gas cleansing building alongside the Co-op where to-day there is that small piece of garden and a seat.

Monica Capadose (née Bramwell)

"My mother Joan Bramwell told me what this job was like. They used to wear overalls and in a vain attempt at keeping the dust and fluff from the scrim out of their hair they worked with scarves tied tightly around their heads. Their fingers were always torn and bleeding and they were never without bits of elastoplast here and there. They worked in shifts, taking over from each other so that the work could go on continuously. The knotted rags were all tied to a very definite colour design - rather like following a pattern for a piece of tapestry. The dust that came off the paint was monstrous. It got into their skin, under their nails, up their noses and into their throats, despite the surgical-type masks they wore. It was thirsty work and my goodness, didn't they need all those cups of our precious rationed tea." Geoff Hoath's mother Esther, (Hetty) had the same memories of that hard work.

"KNITTING IS GOOD FOR THE NERVES 'they' said. But the first enthusiasm for knitting had already begun to ebb when on 1 June 1941 clothes rationing struck it a further blow. After complaints, the government agreed to supply 24 ozs of coupon-free wool a year to anyone wanting to knit for the Forces, though even this came to an end a year later, when only recognised 'knitting parties' were allowed this privilege. The stiff oiled wool we made up into garments for naval men and merchant seamen was terribly hard on the hands and it became more costly when one took into account that thinner wools went further, an important consideration when every 2 ozs 'cost' a clothing coupon. Country children were encouraged to collect whisps of wool from barbed wire fencing around the fields."

Lots of people who could ill-afford to do so, willingly sacrificed precious clothing coupons to make khaki, navy and air force blue garments for the troops. If you knitted for the British Red Cross, the St John's Ambulance, the WVS or the British Legion - they would supply you with wool free of coupons and you took your completed garments to them for prompt dispatch from depots all over the country. Knitting patterns costing 6d or 1/- showed smiling heroes and heroines doing daring things in cable and moss-stitch, thumbs up-lifted in the victory salute. Over ribbed shoulders, aircraft propellers rotated on Spitfires and Hurricanes, and tanks and naval guns protruded with never a hint of a dropped or faulty stitch. Our school like many others 'adopted' a mine-sweeper and teachers were always willing to stay on after school to help unscramble our grubby bits of knitting that had got snarled up. You had to wind your own wool with someone holding the skein out for you, or by putting two chairs back-to-back and winding round them. Sometimes we wrote little notes to the men to put into the toe of a sock.

Don Adams

"Harry Steven, our boss at *Squerryes Farm* - he'd been with an early tank corps during the First World War, so he got to know the officer in charge of that lot, and I got to sit in on one of those tanks - a bit of a change from my Pigmy tractor.

We used to do one night a week on Home Guard duty.Two hours on, one hour off so that there were always two of us on patrol. We slept in bunks in the stables at *Lewins,* (Crockham Hill). If there was a raid on - this was before the Canadians arrived - we used to run out with a spade and bury the incendiaries. There were hundreds of them came down. We pulled them out of the ground and collected them in wheelbarrows, and lots of them never exploded. They were about two feet long with a top or fin on them. They never seemed dangerous to us. We used to enjoy taking them to pieces, cleaning them out and making money-boxes out of them. We used to go miles on foot or on our bikes to collect scrap metal, and we made Christmas decorations out of those strips of silver paper stuff that were dropped by our planes to drift around and confuse the enemy about our radar."

"The Home Guard with their Headquarters at the Drill Hall were much in evidence in Westerham, quite a force of locals and not to be trifled with. Discharging fire arms inadvertently seemed to be a trait and on one occasion Sergeant Mercer was shot in the behind whilst on the rifle range in the Drill Hall. He soon recovered in hospital and was able to laugh about it afterwards, but not for some time.

A Youth Club was formed about mid-war, headquarters at *Winterton House* and watched over by Mr and Mrs Granville Streatfeild. It was well attended and well run, a good thing for the youth of Westerham. And dances were very popular, taking place at St Mary's Hall most Saturday nights and some also at the WI Hall with lessons there also during the week. Elite dances were held at *Pilgrim House*, HQ of the Woolwich Equitable Building Society, on Thursdays, by invitation only from the numerous staff."

In Crockham Hill they had no air raid siren, relying on Westerham's or Edenbridge's to alert them to a raid, according to which way the wind was blowing. They reckoned they came off best - not having that hideous banshee wailing in their midst.

Geoff Hoath

"There was a Wardens' Look-out Post in Squerryes Park, up behind Water

Lane, built by my father Bill Hoath and myself using materials from Durtnells. Only manned at night it had a telephone link to Delagarde Oast House (Headquarters) and the Warden was empowered to sound the siren there. There were bunk beds, a table and chairs and a sand-bagged wall in the front with a plotters' map on the top."

"With the ever present threat of invasion, a road-block was set up near the bottom of Vicarage Hill. A great pile of logs on one side of the road to narrow it down so it could be blocked off by a tree-trunk which pivoted at one end with a cart wheel on the other end to be swung round across the road. It was just near the Red Cow House. My favourite is the little look-out point with slits for two guns overlooking Westerham Churchyard, in the curved wall of the garden of Erlam and Peggy Dobb's house, *Churchgate*, beside the churchyard tool-shed. Facing east-north-east, it commands an uninterrupted view of the approaches to Westerham from that direction as well as of the London Road beyond The Crown.

And in the wall of *Darenth Towers* (now *Westerham Place*) there was a look-out point with 2 gun-holes on the footpath on the way from the A25 to the Market Field."

Peter Steven
"At the beginning of the war there were sentries at the main gate to *Squerryes Court*, at the entrance to the *Farmhouse* and round the back. We grew corn in Wolfe Park opposite the Brewery and a number of bombs fell around us. Of a stick which straddled us, one landed close to the gazebo in Surrey Park, and another on the far side of the hill. My father, who was a Warden in the Home Guard crossed the road to see what damage had been done by yet another that had crashed close to where we kept the chickens. They seemed undisturbed, but he found the cows in that field all gathered around the bomb crater and peering down into it. There was a biggish bomb-hole alongside the A25 and another across the road in a field next to *New Winterton*, in which for some 30 years we grew runner-beans. Bombing had reduced them to a sorry state.

As a 6-year-old when war broke out, I was familiar with the leaky punt in the little boat-house on the lake in front of the Court, and with Bernard Isted collected coot and moorhen eggs from around the lake on a regular basis. The thing was not to get caught by Mrs Warde. We cooked the eggs over fires we lit up in Squerryes woods. The Wardes kept two Jersey cows for their own use and they stored large sealed tins of emergency rations in the Granary, put there by the Ministry of Food against the possibility of invasion."

Peter Finch
"I had a fine collection of metal fragments, including cannon shells, 303 ammunition and quite a number of incendiary bombs, which I was adept at defusing. A lot of these fell and failed to ignite for some reason, so I took them home, as did my friends, we were all souvenir hunters. I did have one mishap up

at the old Tower (in Squerryes) a whole lot fell all around the Tower and failed to go off. I was defusing one and somehow I pricked the detonator by mistake and it blew up in my hand. My whole hand immediately dripped blood and looked quite serious, so I scooted off down the bank to a stream and gave it a rinse. No problem, only about a dozen pin pricks, so I wrapped a hanky round it and went back to collect my treasure. On another occasion I almost set fire to our shed whilst hacksawing a cannon shell in half. I didn't realise it was a 'tracer' until the phosphorus ignited."

"The war taught us kids to scrounge, fiddle and survive. We learnt how to wriggle our way through the chinks in adult pretence. I learnt more about deception and manipulation from the war than I ever learnt facts at school. There was a lot we were up to that we had to hide from our parents which wasn't difficult as they were too busy with the daily grind of blackout, rationing and depressing war news. With my Dad away overseas, my Mum was better not knowing the secret places where we'd got our trophies hidden - some of them highly inflammable and likely to 'go off' if the wrong person should find them. But she won in the end when she gave a whole lot of my trophies to the 'scrap metal drive.'

Of all my treasures, my pride and joy were the nose-cone of a 3.7 inch anti-aircraft shell and innumerable tail-fins from incendiary bombs. We used to swop several of those for other more valuable treasures. If they weren't bent and the paint wasn't chipped they were worth something. But nothing was more prized than a piece of fuselage that had a number or a German word on it, or, most sought after of all, even just A FRAGMENT of a swastika. A black leather *Luftwaffe* flying helmet or goggles or fur-lined mittens were almost beyond price but were harder to explain away. How had we come by such personal property if we hadn't visited a crashed cockpit? Sometimes the soldiers up on the Common would keep something they'd found and give it to us, or they might show us how a thing worked and what a broken piece might have come from."

"When we were home on leave, we often took our army issue boots to Mr Townsend's shoe shop on the corner of New Street and the High Street where Mr Cracknell, a cripple with an orthopaedic boot sat all day making shoes. He used to hand-make for people with foot problems who would travel miles for the comfort of wearing his shoes. He would put our boots on his last and soften the leather with an old bone handle and saddle soap and dubbin or some such. They could be agony those boots, 'specially if they got soaked and then stiff as a board."

Rosamund Brydon (née James)
"There were those who went to ground in an air raid and those who couldn't

bear to miss anything and always went outside and craned their necks to look up at the sky. Jean Urquart (of *Brasted Place*), who spent the war years at *Wheatlands*, Crockham Hill was heard to say:...Don't talk so loud dear, I can't hear the bombs fall."

The state of play as far as the previous night's air raid was concerned, soon began to supplant the usual British obsession with the weather. We all became accustomed to air battles, perhaps of only fifteen minutes duration, yet already parachutes would blossom against the sky to float silently down, giving one time to try to estimate where they might land. Slim logger-headed Dorniers, glinting shark-nosed 109's, slow (we were assured, scantily-armed) Heinkel 111's. A little knowledge might be a dangerous thing but at least this lot surely couldn't be the long anticipated invasion by parachute drop. They didn't look the right type of plane for that.

Geoff Hoath

"We used to ask the Canadians for their Sweet Caporal cigarette packets which we all collected and which carried diagrams of aircraft for identification. Sometimes they'd give us a little sugar too, to 'take home to your Mum', or a packet of fags 'for your Dad', which of course he rarely ever saw!"

"By this stage of the war the landscape was changing. Where only green parkland had been from time immemorial, beneath ancient trees young shoots began to sprout. We got paid £3 an acre to plough up land that had never known a plough before. It was hard work I can tell you and we were sent all over the place to do this."

"Round concrete blocks had been set up by the army at a number of important positions along the A25, on Westerham Green, at Verrall's Corner and at the bottom of Hosey Hill. Had an invasion of this island taken place and military vehicles ventured along our roads, the rolls of barbed wire standing alongside the road blocks would have been unrolled and attached on the other side."

"On 13 August 1940 the newspaper headlines were 'BATTLE OF BRITAIN NOW ON'. First close bombs for us were Farley Common with the death of Mrs Beville. We were all into aircraft-spotting. I remember squadrons of JU 88's or Dorniers, and Flying Fortresses. A Dornier crash near *Pilgrim House*, a V1 near the British Legion and one at Coombe Bank...but most vividly I remember poignantly the aromas of war. Hot metal and oil and burned bodies in the wreckage of crashed aircraft."

"Even to-day, if you know where to look, you can find the blackened stumps in stone and brick walls where, sometimes quite elegant, railings were taken away in 1941. It is said now that it was really an exercise in the whipping up of patriotic fervour set up by the government. Important gates to have survived are those at Peter Finch's *West Lodge* in Quebec Square. Heavy gates that have to be moved rather than just opened. Some people reckon they were left because Ronald Vestey as the meat expert in charge of its distribution for the nation, needed personal protection and that the military therefore left that entrance secured."

Violet Evenden
"I used to buy my nails by the hundredweight and sell them at threepence a pound. Putty like nails was sold by weight and methylated spirit, linseed oil, turps and paraffin were dispensed loose into bottles and cans supplied by customers. Kindling cost tuppence a bundle and accumulators for wirelesses and door-bells were brought to us for recharging. We used to deliver with a small Austin van until the war. After that we used boys on bicycles."

"A number of people who had never done so before began to keep bees. The attraction was perhaps less the promise of honey than the certainty of extra sugar from the Ministry of Food. For bee-keepers soon found that the bees in their hives were perfectly content and productive if one gave them back their own honey whilst keeping their sugar ration for other purposes. Mr Clout of Rectory Lane, Brasted was Westerham's 'bee-man', always willing with his expertise to turn out to help anyone in trouble with a hive or an errant swarm. He knew better than most the improbable rights of owners of bees when it came to the need to venture on to other people's land to recover their swarms. Prompted by the Ministry of Agriculture, he also advised bee-keepers to anchor their hives against over-turning by blast or if a bomb should happen to hit them - in which case they would need to be plugged with chloroform-soaked rags.

People also took to keeping chickens and rabbits. General Lubbock's wife Lettuce of *Glebe House* always laid claim to plenty of scraps from the canteen run by Joan Bramwell of the WVS at St Mary's Hall. It was manned all and every day and catered for airmen from Biggin Hill, the crews of any local barrage balloons and the many troops billeted in and around Westerham. Spam and other sandwiches were made on demand and on a conveyor-belt-system - without benefit in those days of course, of sliced bread. Bill Cosgrove, like many others who had become aware of the rich pickings thrown out by the military, used to take a bucket across The Green to *The Pheasantry* for their scraps for his chickens and rabbits and gave fresh lettuces and greens in return.

From the Canadians at *Compton Chase* and from *The Mount*, commandeered by the military, pig-swill was collected under contract by the Baileys for their market garden at *Mount Lodge* on Westerham Hill."

Ronald Bailey

"I remember my father finding butter and all sorts mixed in with it, and his collecting the swill in dust-bins in a Morris Cowley he had bought for £5 because it had no seats in it. It had a magneto ignition, you could leave it down in the field in the damp and you just swung it to get it started. Those Canadians at *Compton Chase* forgot to 'do' the black-out at the top of the house one night when they were having a party and Jerry responded by dropping a bomb straight down the middle."

Mollie Cosgrove

"The French Canadians had those motorcycle side-car combination things with a Bren gun mounted on the side- car, and if any German planes came down, they would roar through the town on their way to locate them. It was always said that any German crew member who might have survived didn't live for very long if those Canadians got there first. It was also said that however much the Canadians were moved around within the Westerham area, they were always bombed. It was reckoned that there must have been a fifth-columnist somewhere amongst them."

Margaret Tulloch (née Johnson)

"My mother Gladys Johnson along with Olive Darby, Miss Divas, Hilda Lelliott and Doris Wood, ran what the troops called 'The Cosy Canteen' in the hall of our church in Fullers Hill. They only had two burners, washing-up bowls and buckets, and a machine for cutting bread. If they ran out of bread, they just went round to the back of Borehams Bakery on The Green at any time in the evening to get more, and they were often packed out. That canteen fed the first barrage balloon boys to arrive in the district for whom by some error, no rations had been provided. At the end of the evening the Gordon Highlanders or who-ever was there, would send an escort party to see my mother, or the person who was carrying the 'kitty', safely home. But there were some fights, with the Gordon Highlanders on one occasion defending their corner, keeping the women well to the rear, and seeing off some menacing Liverpool lads brandishing razor blades and broken bottles, after a few drinks in the local pubs. Sadly one man was killed."

Beryl Bellingham (née Howard)

"They built a huge NAAFI depot at Moorhouse. All the food arrived on The Flyer and Scammell lorries used to pick it up with Pioneer soldiers working flat out to unload and re-load it. Army lorries used to go to Moorhouse from all over the area, wherever members of the Forces were encamped or billeted, to collect their rations. My parents ran a servicemen's canteen at The Congrega-tional Chapel in Fullers Hill which rivalled the St. Mary's Hall Canteen. It was a very friendly rivalry with the then Minister the Rev. Clifford Pickford (universally known as 'Skip') also much involved and busy helping out with Westerham's Scouts. We used to have musical evenings and if there was an air raid on, we just played and sang even louder."

"They would come and go, those soldiers. This battalion, that battalion. We knew all their badges and where they were from. But we, like them, never knew where they were going. Still that didn't stop us marrying them. They were good neighbours and very generous, those troops from across the Atlantic with their 'Bundles for Britain' that came from Canada and the USA for people who'd been bombed out and lost everything."

Monica Capadose (née Bramwell)
"My mother (Joan Bramwell) used to be taken every week by the NAAFI Manager to buy the stores she needed for the St Mary's Hall Canteen at a depot at Moorhouse. So precious were they that for added safety she kept all the treasured sweets, cigarettes and other tuck to which the forces were entitled, at her own house, *Carter's Cross* in Lodge Lane, where she knew they would not be touched."

"Saturday Night Dances (1s 6d hops) at St Mary's Hall, run by the WVS, were a popular weekly occasion as were those run by the Red Cross to raise money for prisoners of war. These were of particular concern for Westerham people because The Royal West Kent Regiment had suffered badly at Dunkirk, putting many local lads, nearly all of them in the same platoon 'in the bag' until the end of the war. Local farmers too staged dances at the Hall, for Red Cross funds: very popular prizes might be half a pig or a dozen precious eggs. And the National Fire Service band was formed by Norman Peskett, from firemen stationed in Westerham."

June Smith (née Jenner)
"We used to have ENSA (Entertainments National Service Association) performers on Mondays and Fridays to entertain the troops in St Mary's Hall. My Mum used to put them up at home in Madan Road and it was fun having them staying. Old Miss Moffatt a teacher at our school was always trying to get my parents to let me go to London to have my voice trained because 'she has potential'. But in those days it just didn't happen like that, even though one of the ENSA men told my parents 'your daughter has got a voice: you ought to do something about it.' Anyhow I loved singing along with them on the platform. Perhaps I shouldn't say it, but honestly, I thought the war was wonderful. You could have been out every night. We had 2,000 Canadians billeted or camped out up on Limpsfield Chart who might find their way into Westerham in the evenings and at week-ends and they behaved perfectly. They had a lot more money

of course than our lads had, but they would always walk us home very correctly after a dance. And if they gave girls nylons or chocolates which were a treat, they didn't expect anything from us in return."

"Those ENSA people all had ENSA on their epaulets and the men wore a sort of 'uniform' of dark blazer and light trousers."

Joy Lee (née Sutherland)
"A big moment for me was when a group of soldiers carried me shoulder high to an evening performance of an ENSA-type concert given by Eugene Pini and his 'Stars in Battledress.' I had spent a year flat on my back with osteochondritis and was touched to be so carefully man-handled from *Breaches* all the way to St Mary's Hall and back again.

Later, I worked for a year between 1940 and 1941 at the Westerham branch of the Westminster Bank. We had a number of 'troop accounts' with a ledger for military business. And because we were in such a vulnerable area, we had to send carbon copies by post daily of every single transaction done that day, down to Chard to be stored away in the Westminster Bank safe in the Cheddar Gorge."

"The Red Cross Commandant for Westerham was Mrs Harold Streatfeild of *Covers Farm*, Major Warde's sister. The Assistant Commandant was Mrs Eileen Duggan whose home was *Springfields*."

"To squeeze the last ounce out of their petrol ration, some drivers switched off their engines whenever there was a chance to coast downhill in neutral. Others belched and farted their way around on dodgy petrol laced with moth-balls and paraffin with disastrous results."

Don Adams
"Because we Home Guards used to have to go and patrol the railway line every Thursday night, we slept rough in bell tents in the Village Hall at Bough Beech and then we had to walk from Bough Beech, up the railway line, through Penshurst tunnel where we met the tunnelling patrols, and the other way we used to go to Mowshurst. We were looking out for saboteurs or paratroops: the enemy. Our job was to make sure that the line was kept open. We carried those detonators like a black cap that you clip on, that the railway people have, and if we found the line damaged in any way, we were to go several yards up the line and put these on the tracks. When trains came over them they exploded and the drivers knew to pull up. They knew it was us, because we put down four of them. BANG! BANG! BANG! BANG! And they knew there was danger ahead."

Felicity Gladstone
"My father being in command of Crockham Hill's Home Guard, I was

party to their code-name for Bough Beech.
It was *Baker-Baker*: wonderfully *Dad's Army*."

"A German Dornier was shot down close to the West Kent Laundry at Sundridge and four coffins were requested from Westerham Mortuary to be sent to the scene of the crash. But according to a written record of that incident, a fifth coffin was ordered and delivered there the following day when 'too many arms and legs' were discovered in the wreckage. The heads routinely collected by the Special Constables at the scene of crashes did not on this occasion match up with the number of limbs found, nor with the usual number of air-crew for a Dornier. This was the reason for the removal by the police of any heads located at such incidents. Local people claim that it was not so unusual to come upon a policeman walking along, like *Jack the Giant-Killer*, holding one or more heads by the hair."

"Local people were beginning to reckon that enemy pilots were homing in (over them,) on to Biggin Hill, courtesy of the white chalk gashes in the North Downs of the newly-excavated caves behind the evacuated building societies at *The Hill* and *Pilgrim House*. Both were duly dulled by treatment with a chemical dressing."

"My mother was never-ending turning collars and cuffs to get a longer life out of shirts with frayed edges. Elastic soon became almost unobtainable, very weak and liable, literally, to let you down when it 'went'. 'ELASTIC IS SCARCE AND STILL ON WAR SERVICE' a government leaflet announced. But at least it was permissible not to wear and have to darn holes and ladders in stockings. The BARE LEGS FOR PATRIOTISM campaign suited us fine in the summer and it saved us coupons for other garments too. Mum had us girls embroidering ration book protective covers from Dad's old shirts for aunts and God-parents for Christmas and birthdays. Blanket-stitch edging, lazy-daisy for petals, satin stitch for the leaves and French knots for the centres. 'French knots indeed!' my Gran always muttered. She didn't hold with them after Dunkirk."

"My Mum always said she connected certain tunes of what she called 'war music' with certain stages of the war...all that yearning, longing, waiting, for romance, for peace...for the safe return of loved ones. She used to listen to the wireless while she sewed and *Music While You Work* and the *Forces Programme* come to mind. *MacNamara's Band, Jealousy, Moonlight Becomes You, Whispering Grass, Trees*, Glenn Miller's *In the Mood* and Vera Lynn singing *Yours*.

Each period of the war had its own tune. The first winter of the war it was *We're Gonna Hang out the Washing on the Siegfried Line, There'll Always be an England* and *Run Rabbit Run*. She used to sing along with the wireless, and of a

Sunday evening we all had to stand up and not talk during *The National Anthems of the Allies*. But my auntie always sat down when the French Marseillaise began, because they had 'given in' too easily. Yes, I reckon it was the most important piece of furniture we had, that old radiogram. And she used to listen to the everlasting stream of Lord Woolton's numbered 'Food Facts' and recipes from the Ministry of Food on it too."

"For girls like my Mother who loved dancing, (smelling of Bourjois' *Ashes of Roses* or *Evening in Paris*) the war was a happy time in what had virtually become a garrison town, with so many men around in the evenings. Local 'hops' had never been fuller or gayer...all around, couples, on just an hour or so's acquaintance, would be clinging to each other as if to make the most of their last moments of life on earth. She even kept a list of some of the tunes they danced to as each period of the war brought its own.

During the last uneasy months leading up to the war: *Two Sleepy People, Begin the Beguine, Roll Out the Barrel, Three Little Fishes*, and *Little Sir Echo*.

Then as the men went off to France it was *The White Cliffs of Dover, Wish Me Luck as you Wave Me Good-bye, We'll Meet Again, There's a Boy Coming Home on Leave, Its a Hap-Hap-Happy Day, Over the Rainbow...*

When the *Blitz* began in September 1940 it was *A Nightingale Sang in Berkeley Square, When They Sound the Last All Clear, The Last time I saw Paris, I've Got Sixpence, Kiss the Boys Good-bye, I Yi-Yi-Yi-Yi-I Like You very Much* and *Why Don't We Do This More Often?...*

1942 brought *Moonlight Becomes You, It Goes With Your Hair, That Lovely Week-end, Room Five Hundred and Four, Bless 'em All*...and with the Yanks came jiving and jitter-bugging, *Deep in the Heart of Texas, Chattanooga Choo Choo, Don't Sit Under The Apple Tree with Anyone Else But Me* and *Elmer's Tune...*

With the V1's raining down over here, our troops in Normandy were tuning in to the Forces Programme and getting *Don't Fence Me In, Somewhere in France With You, Mairzy Doats and Dozy Doats, Is You Is or Is You Ain't My Baby, We'll Gather Lilacs, We Won't Be Long Out There* and *Imagine Me with my Head on your Shoulder...*

"Some of the tunes, my Mum said, were directly to do with the various stages of the war...like, *Crash! Bang! I Want to go Home, Till the Lights of London Shine Again, Follow the White Line, They can't Black Out the Moon, Where do we go from here? Now That We've Captured Bardia, Oh! What A Surprise for the Duce (they do say, he's had no spaghetti for weeks)...He Can't Put it Over the Greeks...* and *Coming in on a Wing and a Prayer* sung by Vera Lynn in 1943 and credited to one of our pilots landing a badly-damaged aircraft. Dance music by the big bands and orchestras led by Jack Payne, Harry Roy,

263 Company R.A.S.C

GRAND OPENING

DANCE

S. MARY'S HALL

Saturday, July 27

1940

7.30 p.m.

R.A.S.C. DANCE BAND

Admission 1/6.   H.M. Forces 6d.

HOOKER BROS., PRINTERS,

S. MARY'S HALL CANTEEN ENTERTAINMENTS
COMMITTEE

WEDNESDAY NEXT,
20th November
at 7.30 p.m.

GRAND

"SEARCH FOR TALENT"
COMPETITION

Open to All — Soldiers & Civilians

EXCELLENT PRIZES!

Enter your name now to Warens Cycles, Ltd., or
Mr. W. E. Bennett, Newsagent

"Everbody Welcome."   **ADMISSION FREE**

HOOKER BROS. PRINTERS

Geraldo, Joe Loss, Victor Sylvester, Billy Cotton, Mantovani and Henry Hall 'kept our spirits up,' so my Mum always said. And the last waltz was always *Who's Taking You Home To-night?*...danced, eyes closed, cheek-to-cheek or cheek to Brylcreamed head. Followed, as midnight drew near, by *God Save Our Gracious King* and a cautious departure through meticulously blacked-out s-bend exits...many of us surely discovering during the war, for the first time in our lives, the mystic beauty of the night sky or an exciting glimpse of a planet or constellation we'd never noticed before."

"I remember hoarding a precious pre-war cake of wrapped Yardley soap which perfumed a drawer in my dressing-table, a fragrant whiff of better times in a world gone mad with war. I just looked at the wrapper and sniffed the beautiful scent. But nothing would have made me open it. We used to wash our hair in *Drene* or *Amami* and rinse it in rain-water or vinegar.

A Land Army girl who lodged with us used to bring an egg back from work for when she was washing her hair. And she collected pheasant feathers from *Squerryes* to decorate the hat she wore to London when she went home on week-end leave. To me, a school-girl, she had sophistication and 'style'.

And how I envied her her box of Pond's face-powder with its luxurious design of floating fluffy powder-puffs on the lid. And her cut-glass bottle of scent, whose spray with its bulb covered in gold filigree thread she used to aim at her, to me, awesome cleavage before she set off to catch The Flyer."

Peter Steven
"We had four Land Army girls who used to travel round with the threshing gang. There was Daphne (who married into the Gribble family and now lives down Chiddingstone way,) and Betty, and Little Eva and Millie...I think she was."

10 December 1942. SRDC leaflet:

CARP/133/42
Inglewood
Oak Hill Road.
Sevenoaks

Dear Sir or Madam,
It has been reported to the Ministry of Health that at recent lectures the public have been advised to fill, or partially fill their baths, so as to provide a small reserve of water at all times.

Owing to the great waste of water involved, instructors should not give such advice. Instead the public should be recommended to leave in the bath, water which has been used for washing or bathing purposes, but not to draw fresh supplies.

To all Instructors, A.R.P.S., L.A.R.P. and Fire Guard.
Sub-Controller, Edward J. Wilson.
Notices were issued by the Ministry of Fuel to display in hotel bathrooms

AS PART OF YOUR PERSONAL
SHARE IN THE BATTLE FOR FUEL
YOU ARE ASKED NOT TO EXCEED
FIVE INCHES OF WATER IN THIS
BATH.

...MAKE IT A POINT OF HONOUR
NOT TO FILL THE BATH ABOVE
THIS LEVEL.

The Hotels and Restaurants Association willingly distributed this notice for posting in every hotel bathroom, and many had a black line painted around their baths at the right height which came to be called 'the Plimsoll line.' Even the King had 5ins marked on all baths at Buckingham Palace.

The static water tank was an unlovely feature of Westerham green throughout the war years. It is seen here amidst VE Day celebrations before its subsequent removal.

People didn't talk about what they were doing or making

Frederick McCosh: "Francis Cooper remained up at *Betsoms Hill* during the war years. Trained in silversmithing at the Central School of Art and Design in Southampton Row, London, and well-suited to such delicate work, he was employed full time by a South London instrument maker on government contract orders for precision instruments."

In 1942 when Peter Finch went to work at Charlie Sharp's Garage in the motor car section, his Manager Jack Cattaway was away in the RAF.

"Half of the premises was on 'munitions', churning out machined parts for the war effort on a round-the-clock production line. John Igglesden and Reg Myhill were the two foremen in the workshop, each doing a 12-hour shift: one did days, the other nights and there were two other men and four girls."

Pat Wybourne (née Bellingham)
"We swapped around so that sometimes we were on the day shift and then took our turn on the night shift. Some of us used to get ourselves from Sundridge to Westerham, in the blackout and sometimes when an air raid was on, to clock in at Charlie Sharp's on war contract work. From Sundridge Lily Boyle and I usually managed a lift with the wholesaler, Horace Marshall of Fleet Street's delivery van which called at Mr Howe's newsagent's shop in Brasted. Mrs Dick (whose maiden name I can't remember) used to come down from Hosey Hill. She and Mrs Lawrence who are both gone now were part-time workers at Sharps with me. I think our shifts were from 8.00 to 8.00. It was lathe work making spindles of different diameters - using a *vernier* rule and a micrometer - the metal being sprayed with oil against over-heating.

We girls used to wear thin head-scarves to stop the oil from getting to our hair. Oliver Burgess worked there too, on John Igglesden's shift until he went into the forces and so did Joyce Hoath, who became Mrs Slaymaker. We made round brass plates with a hole in the middle for a new gun that was coming out, and Les Gorick who was Manager of the two shifts was delighted when we were highly commended by the War Office for the work that we did here. Charlie's sister Dorothy Sharp worked in the office through the war years."

"Charlie Sharp was a big noise in the ARP. One day he came into the

Sign posts stacked alongside emergency telephone repair equipment (in today's station car park at Oxted, Surrey).

workshop with another man and he was carrying a strange object very gingerly. 'Stand well back everyone', he said, 'this is a butterfly bomb and I am going to immobilize it.' We stood back, at least ten paces and he carefully defused it. On reflection we could all have had our heads blown off."

German butterfly bombs were small innocent-looking anti-personnel bombs, liable to explode with deadly effect at the least disturbance such as being handled or stepped on.

Joan Myhill (née Kimber)

"We had the wives of soldiers who were billeted in Westerham to stay over the week-end. Later, in 1944, in the V1 and V2 days, when my little daughter Pam began shaking every time the siren went, the doctor said that we ought to try to get her away. So I took the three children up to Staffordshire to stay five weeks with one of those wives who had spent week-ends with us in New Street."

"About the middle of the war, we in the Paddock had, I think, 18 fair-sized HE bombs dropped on us, all delayed action, over one night during a raid. Nobody really knew of this until it was daylight. Mr Ayley who lived up the Slip, went to drive off to work at about 6 am, but a large hole in his drive revealed a bomb, unexploded. He just had to get to work so he got a shovel and filled the hole in and drove over it, calling out to his wife that there was a bomb in the driveway and could she tell someone about it. Just close by, either Mrs Austin or Mrs Buckman had one come down the chimney which came to rest in the fireplace. I remember locals were invited up to see it, they all filed through to have a look. Later the BDS (Bomb Disposal Squad) arrived, dug them out and defused them. Nobody was evacuated during this time and I personally watched some of the defusing and later retrieved the acid fuses for souvenirs."

Alan Matthews

"One of our own anti-aircraft shells landed outside my home number 45 London Road, opposite Moreton's Almshouses. It fell right in the middle of the road, shattering the glass in the greenhouses of a nursery garden where the Westerham Press was built after the war."

Gwenda Wood

"I used to cycle from Horn's Hill to work at Evendens. Bob Goose mended things for us in the workshop at the back. He put new bottoms in saucepans, kettles, coal scuttles, coke hods, wheelbarrows and such-like. And he was wonderful at putting new handles on farming and gardening tools and sharpening knives and saws and scythes. He was a proper tin-smith. But he was a bit temperamental. He had a stone back there. But you had to humour him to get him to do what you wanted sometimes. Still you had to have older men in those days.

We were very short of staff and of course you simply couldn't buy a new saucepan or kettle or anything metal as the war went on. Customers needed repairs done and some bought our little cards of 'pop-rivets' for plugging their own. We sold a lot of curtain track and hooks for the blackout. People made extra black curtains and they needed duplication of all the usual fittings for hanging them. Miss Evenden had a blackout screen made and put where the shop door opened so people could sort of creep round it and sidle through without letting any light out. Our proper blackout curtain that opened with the shop door left it unprotected for a few seconds. You didn't want the Warden on to you with his 'PUT THAT LIGHT OUT' for all the neighbours to hear."

"All around us parkland was being ploughed up, school children were 'doing their bit' and men, having been called up and gone off to war were being missed. We seemed to be all old men and women and young children. Nobody had a minute to spare. Everybody was busy with the war. If you saw an innocent bit of green grass, you felt compelled to dig it up and plant something edible in its place."

"My school-boy war was filling sand bags, digging trenches, collecting waste paper, empty jam-jars and scrap aluminium (this on a weekly basis with the Westerham Scouts) collecting acorns for pig feed, digging for victory and poaching rabbits and trout.
RAW MATERIAL IS WAR MATERIAL the posters said. There was never any financial remuneration, nor was it sought, everyone was doing their bit. The scrap aluminium (for aircraft manufacture) along with other material we had collected was stacked high at Winterton House. The paper was inside, the aluminium outside in the adjacent courtyard. I didn't spend much time at home I was too busy with the war."

"Amongst a variety of things, we Guides collected empty cotton reels. The Air Ministry had been in touch with Guide Headquarters with an urgent request for 15,000 of them to be used for a secret job which was later revealed as the insulation of emergency telephone lines. Within one week 30,000 reels had been dispatched, the final total exceeding 200,000. It was just like when 'Blue Peter' asks viewing kids to collect things. Everybody joined in and people wound their thread on to bits of paper so as to give us their reels."

"My memories are of able-bodied men going off into the services, either recruited or voluntarily. An influx of school children evacuees from London, most with no knowledge of the countryside or the rural way of life, particularly after dark. The local cinema (the Swan in Westerham at the bottom of Hosey Hill where to-day is Vulcan Plastics) was about the highlight of entertainment: it was quite busy in the early days of the war. I can only remember one evacuee, Ethel from Camberwell. She must have been a good looker. Everywhere us school children went we carried our cardboard box on a string with our gas mask inside. One never went without them."

Freda McBride

"Our evacuees came to Crockham Hill in the Spring of 1940 in what later came to be known as the 'lull', from the Old Kent Road and Camberwell. They had never wanted to be evacuated and they didn't like it when they got here. It was too quiet, this was before the later activity with raids, VIs and V2s. There were no fish-and-chips shops, no cinemas round the corner, they only wanted to buy groceries in penn'orths or two-penn'orths and they simply weren't house-trained. They were scattered all around Crockham Hill, and they used to come and congregate in front of my parents' shop, and after they'd moved on, we had to hose it down. Everybody complained afterwards that mattresses were spoilt: everything was spoilt. Their facilities at home must have been dreadful. They just had no idea about cleanliness. Most of them only stayed for a week or so. Some of them lingered on for a bit longer and made a war-time life of it. And just one or two are still in these parts to this day and grew up as country folk."

Kev Reynolds now reckons that Crockham Hill's village shop was prob-ably the nearest thing to 'the flesh pots' or real life that was available to them. Pressure had surely been put upon them to leave London which they were as-sured was about to be bombed. When they heard nothing about any air raids, disenchanted and totally unwilling and unable to relate to the vastness of their new habitat, their only thought was to return home. Their behaviour may have been all part of the 'we never asked to come and we don't want to be here anyhow', syndrome.

For a few of them it proved to be just a little outing into the country. Had they come in a large crowd at their own instigation, as many had done for gen-erations to pick hops in Kent, they would have brought their own atmosphere with them. They would also have been earning money, seeing the whole episode as finite and set up by them for themselves along with their families, friends and neighbours. Just a few evacuees, isolated and out-numbered by the locals may have felt threatened and out of their depth from the very first day. Added to which there was the risk of air raid damage to their homes in their absence and war hazards for their menfolk. Many of them clearly felt ill-at-ease and frus-trated and showed it in a variety of ways. Nor, it must be said, were most local people sorry when the decision was made by their visitors to return whence they had come."

Pat Gorick (née Penny)

"We used to have Mr Mavrogordato from *Mariners* come round to sell us National Savings Stamps every week, and I had a Land Army girl staying here who always tried to look the other way as she never had any money to spare.

When the evacuee children were here, Ruth Gadsby who worked at *Lewins* said that the evacuees' parents would arrive down for the week-end as it suited them, whilst the children just squatted down where they were, doing unspeakable things all over the dining-room floor. My next-door neighbour Mrs Cox said that hers wouldn't come to the table as they weren't used to having proper meals but sat on the doorstep eating bread and jam.

A young evacuee mother with a baby was living in squalor in Mrs Slade's gardener's cottage in New Road. Mrs Slade was so horrified that via Mrs Mills she approached the Mills Nanny at *The Oast House* close by, who did her best to help. The baby's pram absolutely reeked and the child was dangerously filthy and at risk. But Nanny came to the rescue with tactful suggestions. She took her some of the Mills childrens' baby clothes and showed her how to bath and feed the baby.

A number of extra people were living at *Heath House (Willy's at Heath)* and the drains clearly couldn't cope with the extra load. One evening during one of the dances at the WI Hall, someone reported a hideous smell outside, and started a rumour of a gas attack. But 'don't panic, don't panic' (just like in Dad's Army,) someone shouted. It turned out that it was just the awful smell from the effluence pouring down the road. But the two Miss Landales who lived in a cottage up New Road were taking no chances. They put their gas masks on and kept them on all night."

"When later on our Kentish kids were evacuated from the country to the seaside (Dawlish in Devon), they didn't have such a different scene to adapt to. Anyhow, we'd landed in France by then and the end of the war was in sight."

Peter Finch

"Food rationing was biting by now; the rations were meagre. The Ministry of Food was churning out recipes to make them go a bit further. And then there was dried egg powder. I liked it, particularly when made into an omelette. But then I liked everything edible, because as a growing lad I was constantly hungry. I would and did eat anything. To supplement our diet we kept rabbits, dozens of them. We gleaned the cornfields and hedgerows to feed them, they helped fill our bellies and my mother made gloves with their pelts.

We indulged in the 'black market' at times, obtaining cream destined for pig food which was made into cheese and helped with the meagre butter ration. A little extra sugar was obtained from a local bee-keeper, and joints of pork now and again from a man who kept a few extra pigs that the Ministry of Food didn't know about. This had to be collected after dark: I remember we didn't want the neighbours to know.

I used to poach a few of the Squire's trout to supplement our rations, until one day PC Cunningham felt my collar when I was fishing in the lake at *Squerryes Court*. He let me off though. One winter's day, after heavy snow and no buses running, I walked with my sister to Edenbridge to collect her milk ration - two pints."

Many people remember that they...

"really enjoyed that dried egg stuff...The troops gave us 'Mullins Whole Powdered Eggs' in tins and 'Maple Leaf Butter.' I think a number of us were very grateful to those Canadian soldiers. We lived better for having them amongst us. Scrambled egg was never so good once you couldn't get powdered egg or 'Klim' or 'National Dried Milk' any more. We'd never known any different and we missed it. I remember tins of Mazawattee tea, 'Hermetically Sealed And Gas-proof' it said on the outside. There was quite a bit of favouritism with the food shops. Those shop-keepers had a fair amount of clout. If they didn't like you - too bad! Mum made jolly good salad cream with liquid paraffin and she used it to fry chips and *spam* fritters, and for making pastry which was easier to handle and wasn't so brittle. The fat ration never allowed for that sort of thing."

But the ever-vigilant Ministry of Food, alerted to what was going on, soon restricted sales of glycerine and liquid paraffin to 'medicinal purposes only', on a doctor's prescription. When Dr Aidan Long arrived to practice medicine in Westerham in 1946, patients were still asking for prescriptions for glycerine and liquid paraffin.

"Posters kept telling you CARROTS KEEP YOU HEALTHY AND HELP YOU TO SEE IN THE BLACKOUT. The carrot was DR. CARROT and then there was POTATO PETE, Ministry of Food characters. We believed everything the government said in those days. I never ate so many carrots and potatoes. And our grown-ups, via the Radio Doctor, were obsessed with the nation's bowels and keeping us all 'regular'."

"I dreaded being told to go and get an egg out of the isinglass in the earthenware crock in a dark cupboard under the stairs. It felt like putting one's hand into a mass of chilly frog-spawn to feel about unseeing for that precious slippery object that simply must not be dropped. I was a fussy, 'picky' child and was turned off by the murky grey colour of the National Loaf which like all the recycled paper, newspapers and books, seemed to get ever grubbier looking as the war progressed."

A school shelter, built by the men of Crockham Hill with help from a company of the Royal Artillery camped in the district. Miss Letchford, headmistress, is at the back.

"The coal ration was full of dust with only some lumps of any size in it. So we kids used to be kept busy of an evening making brickettes of the coal dust with cement powder or earth and water. We got filthy of course, which was hard on Mum, packing it into flower-pots and turning it out once it had 'set'. We thought it was like Mum turning out cakes. The government used to issue communiques every now and again. And one told us to:
'SHARE YOUR FIRES'. Get together with your friends and neighbours and work out a scheme for sharing firesides this winter. One well-warmed room in one house is more sensible and much more comfortable than two rather chilly rooms in separate houses'.. This was good fun and we used to do what they said. I don't know about the grown-ups, but we kids enjoyed ourselves."

Peggy Tulloch (née Johnson)
"In Wilson's Yard where to-day is Fenella Lampshades they were making Bakelite, and material for insulation out of little slivers of fine wafer-like mica on government contract."

Geoff Hoath
"They used to stick them on to boards painted with shellac. They were all shapes of little pieces which were applied like mosaic and sealed with more layers of mica and shellac until finally it was all baked on the spot."

"Some local people can still remember flakes of the mica drifting away from the 'Yard' like snow to settle on neighbouring gardens, as it did on Anthony Brill's parents' garden next-door at *Bincleaves*, now *White Windows*.

"Budding servicemen from about 12 to 18-year-olds were encouraged to join the Army Cadets or the Air Training Corps. The Army Cadets with Major Wells as C.O. used to meet in a hut behind St Mary's Hall (now Westerham Hall), and drill on the playground of St Mary's PNEU School (now Croft Hall School), and the Air Training Corps met at *Winterton House* which was also HQ for the Home Guard under Major Bagnall and which had become very shabby-looking by the end of the war."

Phil Johnson
"Jerry Leslie with Alan Barber and Stanley Dobson started the Scouts in Crockham Hill around 1940-1, and Greville Spencely allowed us to use his swimming pool at *Spenceley's* in Goodley Stock every Wednesday....I suspect that that weekly bath did us all no harm!"

Bill Combley
My father Jim was one of the first to volunteer for the LDV whose head-

quarters was in Winterton House. I remember them opening cases of rifles that came from America. They were packed in hard grease that took a lot of getting off: in fact to get the grease out of the barrels they pushed red hot iron rods down them. They also made loads of Molotov Cocktails out of old beer and wine bottles filled with a mixture of petrol, oil, paraffin, creosote and tar, in fact anything that would burn. There was a bit of string or wire round the neck to tie a squib to, which was to set the mixture alight when the bottle burst as it hit the target.

Phil Johnson
"My sister Marjorie used to play the piano for the weekly dances at Crockham Hill and round about. She married a merchant seaman from the Seamens' Convalescent Home on Limpsfield Chart who had been rehabilitated from a prison camp having been sunk by the *Scharnhorst* in 1940. As members of the Crockham Hill Scouts Troop we used to tour and give Gang Shows to such places - wounded everywhere. How innocent we must have seemed."

Marjorie Thomson (née Johnson)
"Phil, aged about 13 or 14 used to play his ukelele and sing a song or two, *a la* George Formby!"

Joy Lee (née Sutherland)
"My mother 'Millie' Sutherland was O.C. of the Girls' Training Corps with help from Anne Warde. Mr Clarke, O.C. Air Training Corps who lived at Biggin Hill, co-operated with them and helped with drill etc."

Monica Capadose (née Bramwell)
"We wore white shirts and navy-blue knickers and we felt we looked like Wrens."

Joan Thorneycroft (née Lelliott)
"We wore navy-blue skirts, white shirts, black ties and navy-blue forage-caps."

Olive Darby (née Hazel)
"They were training us to be ready to go in the forces. We used to meet at the WI and march about in the old Market Field outside, with a sergeant drilling us and tapping our hands into the right position. We went to Squerryes Court one day for tea and she gave us boiled eggs. But we were all frightened to start in on them because we didn't know what to do. Ought we to crack the top and peel the shell off, or take the tops off with our knives?"

"To keep local girls occupied, off the streets and safe from the many young soldiers loose around the town, Hilda Baker (later Sandal) used to run weekly ballroom dancing classes in her big front room above their Westerham Dairy shop, next to the Post Office, where to-day is Castle Antique Centre."

June Smith (née Jenner)
"Victor Sylvester: marvellous! With the old gramophone to wind up and those needles to change. Oh, the fun that it all was."

And with the same aim in view, Mrs Bill Cosgrove invited local girls once a week into her home, behind her sweet shop on the Green, to help them with dressmaking and hairdressing. She was also an 'ARP Housewife on the Green', prepared when the siren went to take anyone and everyone into her shop. Children were offered Jelly Babies and grown-ups all got a cup of tea and a biscuit to calm their nerves as wooden shutters were hurriedly fixed in position to stop shattered glass from falling out on to the pavement."

At Crockham Hill Rosemary Whittaker-Browne aged sixteen, whilst living at *Hurst Farm* with Tom and Constance Steven, also started a little dancing class, in the WI Hall.

"It was really to help occupy the evacuee children and give their hosts a break. They used to come to me straight from school, just popping down the lane, and it became very popular. I wasn't qualified as a dancing teacher of course at that young age, but I had been trained in dancing and deportment at the John Tiller Academy in Cambridge Circus which had produced the Tiller Girls, Jessie Mathews, the Dare sisters and others. They taught ballet, deportment, tap-dancing etc. and generally gave you 'poise'. I just thought that those little kids might benefit, and certainly it helped occupy them for a while after school. The class carried on after the children had gone back to London, with me teaching even great big lads from farming families round about. Henry and Bob Steven, Denis Skinner and Gordon Edgar were amongst those who came a number of times and were no doubt sent to me by their parents to help them to acquire poise and to learn how to dance.
One ten-year-old evacuee girl whose father was a tailor in the East End was particularly good. She wrote to me once she was back in London, and of course they all went back after only a limited time, thanking me for her lessons. I had a very tall elegant man, Philip Spencer, who was a superb dancer to help me with the classes. I believe he was chauffeur to the Lattas at *Newlands*."

Ted Ivey
"Mr Churchill's great roll of newspapers from all over the world used to come on the down train every Sunday morning and someone from *Chartwell*

would come and collect them. My mother-in-law had Mr Churchill's policeman lodging with her in Madan Road. We (at Westerham Station) always waited for people if we could see them coming, and we didn't like hurrying passengers up if they were saying their good-byes. Occasionally we'd have to go back if we'd just pulled out level with the signal-box and someone was hurrying along. During the war we used to stop to drop two little girls off at some farm cottages at *Charman's Farm* where the cattle bridge is now, over the M25. Those cottages were demolished to make the motorway. We didn't want the kids to have to walk home from the station in the blackout.

On Wednesdays and Saturdays we had what was called 'the theatre train'. The last train from London used to reach Dunton Green at about 12.20 and would be met by The Flyer which would pick up anyone (sometimes it was only one or two passengers) for all stations to Westerham. It was to fit in with the matinees and an evening out afterwards...and all for 2s 11d each way - with me selling the tickets and/or acting as signalman. This went on just the same all through the war when a Dunton Green return was 1s 4d for a train-ride with light bulbs painted dark blue and carriages without any heating.

A chap called Jack Withell from Lee Weller's Garage in the London Road was the driver of the lorry that used to pick things up at the station for delivering all around the town and out to the pubs and farms. Anything for Brasted was sorted out and taken back along the line.

For weighing goods and cattle to do with the market we had the weigh-bridge alongside the goods shed which took just the one truck with a big crane for loading and unloading. Lots of coal arrived for domestic use and for the gas-works in the Croydon Road, and the RAF lads used to come down from Biggin Hill to collect ammunition which came by train - to take back up Westerham Hill with them. We weren't allowed to touch those trucks full of great shells and suchlike.

Where to-day are the Police Houses at the top of Madan Road and round in Sandy Lane, there were masses of troops in that open space, their officers billeted in *Oak Lodge* (now gone), with their great anti-aircraft guns. It was a kind of depot for them, and during the raids on London they used to tear around the countryside to various positions and blaze away.

In the signal-box we had a little cooker and the kettle on the go. But later in the war, nobody ate so well as our three Italian POW's: they fed better than any of us. They'd come up into the signal-box with ½lb lard and fry whole tins of corned beef or spam, when we only had 3 ozs meat a week each. They used to help around the station yard and with the loading and unloading. We had Joan Bowen and Ivy Terry too, young married Westerham women who did portering at the station, dividing the day into shifts between them.

Those POW's brought their own real Italian coffee too, and made it there on the hob in the signal-box, and sometimes they gave us a cup. We supposed it was all standard POW issue and that they had to be properly looked after. They were good lads though. Of a blacked-out night in my signal-box I had my knitting to pass the time. My wife used to start me off with a sock. Then I just went on round and round. She turned the heels for me, then on I went again with my four small needles. I was alright if I just kept on going the right way round. All that's left of Westerham station to-day is an orange-painted iron stump, the base of that crane, standing about six feet high in The Flyer's Way."

Attempts have been made again and again to drill or dig out that iron base, but it has always defeated 'them' and now stands, in the good company of three nice young trees on a well-kept piece of grass.

"The war was fun unless somebody near to you got killed. To occupy my mind as I stood by the white line painted to mark the edge of the platform, I used to read the war-time regulations on the wall of Westerham station:-

DURING BLACK-OUT HOURS - FOR YOUR OWN SAFETY:
KEEP ALL BLINDS DRAWN. KEEP ALL WINDOWS SHUT
except where it is necessary to lower them so that
passengers may open doors to alight.
MAKE CERTAIN
that the train is at the platform, and that you alight
on the platform side.
WHEN LEAVING THE CARRIAGE
close windows, lower blinds again, and close the door
quickly.
ALL UNNECESSARY LIGHTS
will be switched off in the event of an Air Raid
warning.

I came to hate Westerham Station. So many partings and saying good-byes that might be your last, whilst others averted their eyes. I wasn't sorry when they pulled it down. It held too many memories for me."

"Some people who don't know any better, think that the road now called 'The Flyer's Way' is named after all those airmen who flew in and out of Biggin Hill over Westerham during the war. But of course it isn't. It commemorates, as does 'Railway Terrace', the little train of the Westerham Valley Railway and its station that occupied that part of the town from Wednesday 6 July 1881 until its closure on Saturday 28 October 1961."

"The *Blitz* was disastrous for many London theatres which, with their audiences gone, simply closed down and transferred their productions to the provinces. Only *The Windmill* ladies, a great wartime institution, 'never closed.'

*" The Flyer would be waiting to fetch us home to Westerham." This photograph
shows the train at Brasted Halt.*

But after May 1941, when the West End theatres re-opened with the last performances starting at six, one was out into the blackout by nine. We used The
Flyer to go up and down and saw some excellent shows. *The Dancing Years, The
Corn is Green, Black Velvet, Ten Little Niggers, The Lisbon Story, Arsenic and
Old Lace, Pink String and Sealing Wax, Uncle Harry, Acacia Avenue, No Med-
als* (in praise of the wartime housewife), *Dear Brutus, Blithe Spirit* and *While
the Sun Shines*...and always at Dunton Green The Flyer would be waiting, pant-
ing with steam up, to fetch us home to Westerham."

"There was a camp for Italian POWs in the woods on the right-hand-side,
all the way up the Rips from where to-day is Redlands at Moorhouse to
Broomlands Lane, by the bus stop at the top on the way to Oxted. Richard
Brayne of Thriftwood Cottage dug up a pistol in his garden there when planting
some shrubs. Westerham had Polish troops too, and to this day there are a number
of Westerham women whose husbands are Polish and are still living in these
parts."

"In 1941 the Red Cross and St John's Ambulance took over the big house at *Combe Bank*, rent-free from the 'Society of the Holy Child Jesus' for 'the duration', as an RAF convalescent hospital. All around the house and grounds RAF personnel were kept busy recovering crashed aircraft, 'ours' and 'theirs'. Dismantling for spare parts and scrap metal went on there and on the small historic First World War air-field and in its hangers close by at *Dibgate Farm* on Chevening Road Sundridge. These were also used by the RAF's No 86 Maintenance Unit for servicing Spitfires."

The air-field was originally laid-out in the early years of the 20th Century by Robert Mond, the famous industrialist chemist associated with ICI who lived at *Combe Bank House.* When, in 1910, he sponsored the manufacture of aircraft by a Polish aviator Prince Serge de Bolotoff the hangers were constructed. A number of biplanes were built there and flown by Test Pilot Lieutenant Olechnovitch and others, before aircraft production ceased in about 1919.

The airmen who worked at *Combe Bank* during WW2 were billeted in a number of private homes around Westerham and Brasted, with the Bill Cosgroves having some of them staying at their home on Westerham Green. Mollie remembers that they might have several at a time and that her mother offered a double-room if one was available, so that wives could join their husbands for a brief visit.

Beryl Bellingham (née Howard)
"My father, Harold Howard was a billeting officer with Sir Henry Pelham and my parents always offered a double room when they could. My husband and I are still in touch with one of the RAF men who stayed at Number 10 The Paddock in those days. He worked at the M.U. (Maintainance Unit) at *Combe Bank* and, unbeknown to us of course at that time, he had picked up one of the very first VI doodlebugs, which he took to Sundridge to be dismantled and examined."

Every Friday was dance night at Crockham Hill. In this village the hall was loaned by the Women's Institute,whose members ran the canteen. On the left hand side, Mrs Pat Gorick, to the right Mrs Stubbings.

Everyone had 'gone to it' and got down to war

*F*OR ARP Wardens.......*I suppose the training was the same all over the country, so many lectures, a written examination and a pass out card. In 1939 the only weapon that Hitler was expected to use against us was poison gas, and very little was heard of high explosives and incendiary bombs. I shall never forget the issue of Gas Masks in September 1938, everybody fitted, measured...the pressure so great that almost everybody was treated as medium size and the respirators were handed out like hand-bills.*

In September 1939 the late Mr E. A. Taylor was Sector Warden for my area (Westerham Hill), and Mr Crapp was Parish Head Warden...The Sector Post was at Plovers, Pilgrims' Way. There were 40 people living at The Hill and it was suggested that I be specially responsible for the building and thereby relieve the local Wardens...

Sector Warden Colin Dence struck me immediately as being full of enthu-siasm and I think a little impatient of our shortcomings...(Warden) Compton Skinner gave us hospitality, kept the minutes and details of the equipment that was not there...

When the Compulsory Fire Watching Order came into force we had more experience of Dence's fire and water drill...I doubt if the residents of Pilgrims' Way could before the war have imagined themselves going along on Shanks' pony to Hill School armed with buckets, axes and stirrup pumps.

Bill Thomas

"My father 'Tommy Thomas' and my mother who throughout the war years ran the 13-bedroomed George & Dragon Hotel as it then was, remembered that in May 1940, Queen Wilhelmina of the Netherlands stayed at the hotel and signed her name in the visitors' book which in those days all residents had by law to do. Holland had been invaded by the Germans just at that time, so she must have been on her way from the coast into exile".

Farley Croft, a large private house where to-day is the residential area known as *Farley*, was opened on 17 October 1939 as a hospital for sick evacuee children billeted in the district.

Mollie Cosgrove

"They arrived by train and their parents visited them, travelling to and fro on the Westerham Flyer. There were a number of caring Jewish relatives who visited assiduously - which sadly some did not. *Farley Croft*'s first Matron was a Miss Coombs, and housekeeper Lilian Hay, (Dr Hay's wife) with two full-time nurses. I worked there from 1941-1944 when at Dr Hay's suggestion I went in January 1945 to work for him at his *Borde Hill* surgery on Vicarage Hill. Later, *Farley Croft* was closed for a short time until it reopened to be taken over by Barnardos."

"In 1940, going to school was optional because of the air raids. My school report dated 1942, my final one, showed me as having been absent 49 times that last term. By this time the air raids had quietened down a bit so there was no real excuse for not going. My mother must have let me off because of the war, but I had plenty of things to occupy my time."

Some motorists had their cars commandeered and many were forced by lack of petrol to lay theirs up. The RAC recommended washing the exterior, reducing the tyre pressures to half-pressure then removing them, draining the radiator, removing the sparking plugs, pouring a teaspoonful of engine oil into each cylinder, turning the engine by hand and then restoring the plugs and finally mounting the car on blocks of wood beneath the axles, there, emasculated to await the defeat of Hitler. Dr Winder remembers that his big coach-built Morris Cowley was dealt with in this way when it went into store at Charlie Sharp's garage for the years he was away in the army.

Branded petrol was replaced on the outbreak of war by 'pool', a blend said to be superior to peacetime 'No 3' grade, though inferior to premium fuel. Although it was known to be illegal to supply it to customers who came with portable containers or to store it without a licence, people were soon scurrying around Westerham with empty cans, buckets and bottles. 'Pool' cost 1s 6d a gallon, then raised to 1s 8d and later to 2s 1½d. Black Market petrol at 6s 6d was in the early days not too hard to come by, though commercial petrol was soon dyed a distinctive red. But the word went round that this tell-tale dye could be eliminated by pouring the petrol through an ordinary gas-mask's charcoal filter.

Every car-owner was entitled to a basic ration of petrol, the coupons being obtained by presenting the car log-book at any post office. A varying number of 'supplementary' petrol coupons were issued for essential business or domestic purposes to anyone who could prove that the basic ration, based on the size of the car, was not adequate for legitimate needs. Doctors, district nurses, farmers and vets were fortunate over petrol.

Motorists had from 1939, to paint the bumpers and running-boards of their cars white, from May 1940 were forbidden to have a wireless in the car (even an unfixed one) and from June 1940 were compelled to immobilise the vehicle, if leaving it anywhere except in a locked garage - usually by removing the rotor arm or the main ignition lead.

Nevertheless, two good things did happen for motorists. Driving tests were suspended on the outbreak of war, and a wartime 'National Service Licence' was issued to all applicants, and though tests were resumed in January 1940, they were dropped again that summer. For the rest of the war learners were able to drive alone and without 'L' plates. And because of the blackout and dimmed head-lights, there was a general introduction of white lines down the middle of the road which had been the exception before the war.

Gwenda Wood

"At Evenden's we couldn't get more than just a few batteries so every time we had a delivery there used to be a stampede. They'd all want the number 8's for their hand torches, but we had to ration them - one to each customer. Miss Evenden was strictly fair about this. The airmen came down from Biggin Hill for some things, razor-blades and suchlike. They had the NAAFI of course, but there weren't more than just a handful of shops up there in those days. It wasn't developed, you really couldn't call it a village. Like Tatsfield it was more like a little shanty Wild West place. We sold pink paraffin which we had to ration too. They brought their own cans for filling up. People used to put some in their cars and some special tablets too, to make the petrol go further. The pink was for Valor stoves. But the police used to notice the smoke coming out of the back of the cars if people added paraffin to their petrol".

Dr Winder says that the little tablets people used to put into their tanks to remove the pink colour in their illicit petrol were *Phenobarbitone* or *Luminal*.

"Gas masks were good for making rude noises and to get the colour out, my Dad used his to strain his petrol through the charcoal filter in the snout."

"When the Battle of Britain started I didn't really go to school at all. I think it was optional at that time. At Hosey they used to drag all the desks together for the kids to get under them. But I liked to see what was going on and I didn't want to miss the dog-fights. We lived in the Paddock at that time. They were very exciting times for a boy of my age. The first real scare I had of the war was round about the 13th August 1940 when bombs were dropped on Farley Common".

John Warde

"My mother told me that during the Battle of Britain a German plane crashed in the back yard at *Squerryes* and when the wreck was being removed they asked her what she wanted from it and she said 'the swastika'. But we've never been able to find it and reckon it must have been pinched during all the repairs that had to be done to the house. A pity really as it would have been nice to have it on display here as part of the history of the house.

In 1941 after my father had returned from Dunkirk, he travelled around the country and then had a battery of guns along the Norfolk coast. So we moved up to Sheringham until 1943 when we came home to *Squerryes*. Lots of incendiary bombs fell on the estate with the sand-pit near *Covers* seeming to be a favourite target. I understand that a number of German bombers weren't too keen on going on to face London with its anti-aircraft guns, so flew up and down this valley, just short of their target, making up their flying time, using up fuel and dropping their bombs before returning to their bases having apparently done their duty.

There were a number of strange sticks of bombs around here. One landed in the lake, another up near the gazebo, one in the park at the back and another in *Lodge Park*, south of the old reservoir. That line of craters is still there though on pasture land some of them were filled in at the time. A number of them also fell on Westerham Woods and several landed on *Force Green Farm*."

Don Adams
"Farm workers during the war had a few privileges. We got an extra cheese ration and permits for thermos flasks. You couldn't just go out and buy thermos flasks in those days if you didn't have a permit. I used to issue them to the farm labourers who brought one back that was broken. The tractor used to shake them to bits, or the horse would take a step forward, knock the flask to the ground - and then tread on it. Miss Evenden could never understand how it was that I kept coming back with all those broken thermos flasks and permits for new ones. But there were a number of farm workers who couldn't get in to get theirs, and as I worked at Squerryes Farm and had my dinner (1s 6d) at the British Restaurant (where to-day is the Thai restaurant, next to where Bill Thomas's shoe shop is), I passed Evendens on my way."

The Control of Paper Order, May 1940.

No person shall in connection with...any sale by retail, wrap or pack with paper any article which does not reasonably require such wrapping or packaging for its protection...

Gwenda Wood
"At Evendens, as everywhere else, people brought their own paper for wrapping things up. I was really clerical. But as time went by I worked in the

shop helping out. I did the book-keeping and all that wretched purchase tax which had to be absolutely correct, upstairs in a little sort of cupboard off Miss Evenden's big room.

There was no 'new' building going on in those days, but firms needed supplying for repairing air-raid damage. Most of our account customers were builders. We had very few accounts for me to deal with for the public during the war, because there were so many things you just couldn't buy - which is why I was able to help out in the shop.It really was a good time for the little builders: without the young men who had been called up, a number of older men with small firms did work on ceilings that had fallen down. One lad who used to come from Brasted to work at Evenden's was killed in the Air Force and Leslie Carpenter who travelled to Westerham from Redhill every day, he went into the Air Force too: but he came back after the war."

Edna Peake

"I was eighteen when war broke out and was evacuated to Westerham with the Woolwich Equitable Building Society. The arrival of our records from London was chaotic as the lorry overturned taking the corner at the top of Pilgrim Lane, spilling all the addressograph department things into the driveway. All the records of shares, mortgages etc. on little plates for printing dividend warrants and tabs and such like. We had to sort them all out before we could move in. We used to have to sleep in a huge shelter they had had cut out under the North Downs - until we got brave and fed up with going down there, taking our mattresses with us to sleep amongst all those 'dirty deeds' as we used to call them. A number of us caught fleas from being down in that shelter and were devastated. Nurse Ford came up to see to us.

In June 1942 I joined the Land Army as I had always intended volunteering for war work and wanted to work with animals in the country and I stayed in it until October 1948. In time I got one of Jack Stevens' cottages in Duncan's Yard and I delivered milk for *Force Green Farm* with a pony and cart. I had to look after the pony and carried pint and half-pint measures as well as bottled milk. Every other week I used to have to go into the dairy where we did all the washing, sterilizing and bottling at the farm. Mr Steven came to my rescue when a German POW working at *Force Green Farm* used to lie in wait for me in one of the cow-sheds and leave me little billets-doux."

Bob Wood

"We were issued with stirrup-pumps and we garaged the light trailer fire pump for the National Fire Service people at *Force Green Farm* and we had training on that. Any soldering we needed done on farm equipment or for sharpening saws and such-like we took them to Bob Goose at Evenden's. Heavy farm machinery we took to Bert Verrall and his brother and Mr Chapman at the blacksmith at Verrall's Corner, or to 'Alf' Nicholas opposite The Standard."

Mrs Darkin who before the war ran St Mary's PNEU School (now Croft Hall School), behind St Mary's (now Westerham Hall), had her premises commandeered by the Army. She moved with her children to the British Legion Hall in Mill Lane, returning after the war to find her playground a mass of barbed wire. In 1948, some rationing was still in force and school lunches were wheeled by truck from the British Restaurant up the London Road, by school boys in their lunch-hour.

The brass hand-bell used in the school to-day has ARP stamped on it, and at the base of the wooden handle the words FIDDIAN, and J.B. 39 engraved on a metal band. This bell is an on-going link with the war years during which a number of Westerham men still remember that they paraded and drilled on the then rough earth of a childrens' school playground.

Gladys Ivey (née Whitmore)
"You had to take Air Force men or evacuees. I had only been married for three months and I didn't want any other man in my house, so we got this brother and sister: Doris was about eleven years old and Gordon was three, and they were lovely children. They stayed with us for quite a long time and went to Westerham schools, and my Mum and Dad had another brother and sister evacuees just down the road, so Mum helped look after them all. But they had gone back to Camberwell by the time we had the rocket on Madan Road in 1945. We came to know their parents quite well and they thought the world of us. We kept in touch for quite a long while, but then we lost contact."

Gladys Ivey herself, with her little boy, was to become an evacuee once the flying bombs began to arrive.

Sonia Williams (née Mavrogordato)
"At *Mariners* at Crockham Hill, we had three reluctant evacuee mothers and their three small children. But they all returned to Camberwell whence they had come, after only three days. They had not wanted to leave London in any case."

Felicity Gladstone
"In September 1939 our father had returned on business to *Lewins* from Scotland where all the rest of us still were, towards the end of our school summer holidays. When we all arrived back at Crockham Hill we found him surrounded by three evacuated families each with three small children already established. They were very early evacuees and I remember taking some of the children out into the garden where one of them promptly fell into the pond and

another to my astonishment and dismay turned out not to be wearing any knickers. A boarding-school thirteen-year-old, I had never come upon such a thing before and was slightly shocked. They didn't stay very long and soon began to drift back to London." Others remember that the little evacuees were apt to 'stick' on playground slides because of their lack of knickers.

We used to bicycle up to swim at Sir Percy Mackinnon's at *High Quarry* and I remember from up there, when the siren had gone and it had been pretty noisy, my father and Sir Percy sending us off to their air raid shelter. But we were soon allowed to join him and my father to watch the dog-fight that was going on and to see one of our planes doing a splendid 'victory roll' against the background of a brilliantly blue sky. All four of us were school-age children so it was all just very exciting for us.

We had various regiments stationed in Crockham Hill, notably the French Canadians who played tennis on our lawn. Some of them were billeted across the road at *Crockham Hill House* which became a Youth Hostel later, after the war. Once the French Canadians had gone we had a Cheshire Regiment and we used to have their wives staying with us at *Lewins* at week-ends so that they could be together a little. At times we had no idea how many people we had in the house. We had an old cook called Ruth and the men used to go to her and say 'can we come and stay in your house?' So it wasn't done through my mother and we used to find people all over the house. On one occasion when my father was travelling back from Sevenoaks to Westerham and picked up a man who was hitch-hiking, he said: 'and where are you staying?' To which he replied:'with you sir'."

———————————

"Sometimes passing soldiers would join in our ball games, and it might be several minutes before we got our ball back. One of them coached us and taught us to be more adventurous with our footwork. They said they missed their own kids back home."

Malcolm Taylor
"We used to play with old hoops or bicycle wheel frames and old tyres in Madan Road, bowling them along and attacking each other. The large lorry tyres were bombers and the smaller ones fighters as we advanced, trying to get through the enemy."

"There were three kinds of shelter.
The 'public' shelter, of which Westerham had one where to-day is the entrance to Delagarde Road where used to be 'Mo' Baker's *Delagarde Farm* in the Croydon Road and one at the bottom of St Mary's Churchyard - which was virtually never used as it was permanently full of water."

Then there were shelters of a sort for a small number of children at St.

Mary's Infants, St. Mary's Girls and up at Hosey Boys' School."

The 'Anderson' was the most widely used domestic shelter at the height of the *blitz*. Named after Sir John Anderson, Cabinet Minister with special responsibility for Air Raid Precautions, by September 1940 more than 2,300,000 had been distributed. They arrived as curved sheets of corrugated iron that had to be bolted together and sunk in a pit 3ft-4ft deep, then covered with a thick layer of earth. Some Westerham residents had these where space in the garden allowed, one of which still exists at number 30 South Bank.

The 'Morrison' (indoor 'table') shelter - named after the Home Secretary and Minister of Home Security Herbert Morrison - became available to householders in 1941. By day many people used them as dining tables, and slept in the oblong steel boxes, the modern equivalent of a four-poster with their mesh sides, at night.

"Kids felt very secure in them and kept their favourite toys down there amongst the bedding. It was a place to retreat to not only during air raids but in any kind of crisis, out of sight, safe and comforting. There's nothing quite comparable for a troubled child to-day."

Daisy Taylor (née Fuller)
"We used ours in Madan Road as the main table for meals, doing homework, and everything, in the middle of the room. But when the siren went, we couldn't all fit in. My husband and the two children managed it, but I was left outside, pregnant, bulky and unable to join them."

"We really had no garden, just a yard filled with our Anderson. So we planted vegetables all over its hooped top. And when there was an air raid on, Mum made us put cotton wool in our ears and a pencil rubber between our teeth so that even if we'd been killed, we wouldn't have been deafened."

"Our Morrison was like a big iron table and good for ping-pong - even when my little sister was asleep underneath it, surrounded by stout wire netting."

Walter (Jumbo) Gammage
"I still use my Morrison, out in the garden now, with a vice on it. It's splendid for holding, cutting and filing pieces of sheet metal or metal piping."

Lots of people remember that after the war their cats continued to occupy the cosiness of their 'table' shelter, children played at 'houses' in theirs and that

they made splendid rabbit hutches if you could persuade your neighbours to he
you get the heavy thing outside.

"Public shelters were huge square grass-covered mounds with air vents
top. We used to spend hours rolling down their steep sides and we went
playing Cow-boys and Indians around the corners, because when we tried pla
ing British and Germans, nobody would ever 'be' the Germans."

John Warde
"At *Squerryes* the Military Police had the top storey where they put
bunks and ablutions and we could hear them moving about. We kept to the
end of the house with all the enormous kitchens and so on in the wing which
now been pulled down. So we lived there most of the time and there was als
hut in the garden in which a lot more furniture was stored. The army built a lo. __
breeze-block out-buildings, where the old laundry used to be, for their loos and
showers.

The stable yard was covered over and became a REME workshop: on the
wall overlooking the lake you can still just see 'Section 1,2,3 etc.' painted on the
wall. There were vehicles all parked down there and there's still a concrete foundation where they had Nissen huts. Those we pulled down in the early 1950's.
And there were two Nissen huts down by the lake which were cook-house ones
in which they ate."

"There was always a mad rush to buy pipe-cleaners which made quite
good hair-curlers, which we couldn't get, no more than there were any kirby-
grips, hair-pins or even combs for most of the war. It was first come first served
but only one each of everything, specially number eight torch batteries. Government posters made everyone hate the 'Black Market' - but nobody knew what a
'black-marketeer' looked like. I suppose it was the early days of things 'falling
off the back of a lorry'. Mums seemed to queue for hours. If it was in short
supply it had got to be worth queueing for...though sometimes you didn't know
what it was till you got to the head of the queue."

There was a category of volunteers called the Housewives Service whose
members undertook a variety of unspectacular jobs behind the scenes to help
others during the war years. Darning soldiers' socks was one of the commonest
of such jobs. Their front windows sported an official HOUSEWIVES SERVICE
sign.

"At the Bill Cosgrove's shop on the Green during much of the war, notices on the window said: SORRY NO SWEETS, NO CIGARETTES AND NO
ICES...or like so many shops: SOLD OUT. Instead of being as busy as pre-war

The canvas water tank (or dam) on Westerham Green seen after the days of the worst shortages, reflecting Mrs Bill Cosgrove's sweet shop and 'cream ices' for Victory celebrations.

with her confectioner's business, Mrs Cosgrove nearly always had a house-full of 'air boys'. Very often these were lads who worked at *Combe Bank* at Sundridge on the recovery and dismantling of crashed aircraft, both friendly and enemy. They used 'Queen Marys', sixty-foot-long transporters that could accommodate entire planes, to pick them up, but they were a nightmare to meet up with in our narrow country lanes."

CANADIANS IN COURT. TOOK CAR WITHOUT CONSENT

At Sevenoaks Police Court on Wednesday, before Mr A.G. Anderson and Mr Alec Young, three Canadian soldiers admitted taking and driving away a car from Westerham the previous evening, the property of Dr Anthony Winder, without the consent of the owner.

Evidence was given that the car was left outside the owner's surgery about 10.45 pm on Tuesday, and was missed about 11 pm. Later PC Cunningham and Head Special Constable Peter Knight saw the car coming towards them near Limpsfield. They gave chase and approximately half-a-mile away the car was found ditched. The three men were found in a ditch nearby. The three men were handed over to the military authorities to be dealt with.

Dr Winder

"Joe Cunningham, our local policeman joked with me because I'd clearly omitted to remove my rotor arm as I should have done to immobilise my car. Had the culprits not pleaded guilty and I been required to answer questions, my misdemeanour would surely have been commented upon". But Rosamund Winder still has touching memories of the thoughtfulness and sensitivity of PC Cunningham who lived at Westways.

"He was so considerate that if there was a burglary, to spare their feelings, he used to fold all the ladies' scattered underwear and put it back in their drawers before the owners went into their bedrooms."

At Crockham Hill the new Vicar the Rev Oliver Fielding Clarke arrived in 1940 but was unable to move into the vicarage.

...While it was standing empty the army had moved in and occupied it. This, as we discovered afterwards, was quite contrary to the law on requisitioning, but it took months to get the troops out and they left the place in a very bad state...Various people kindly took us in as paying guests till we got the vicarage back...We could not return to normal service times till I had raised some money to have the church blacked-out in the evenings after sunset and in the dark winter mornings...the parish was very scattered, and soon petrol rationing became so severe that I could no longer afford to keep the car on the road and had to walk or use a bicycle.

The Rev. Charles Steer, Rector of St Peter's Limpsfield recorded that:

The early part of the year 1940 was quiet, but with the fall of the whole Western European Coast into German hands, things became much more dangerous and exciting in the early summer. With the immediate prospect of invasion in June, troops were rushed to battle positions in depth behind the coast...The first Canadian Division occupied the line from Crockham Hill westwards, with the Edmonton Regt. and Princess Patricia's C.L.I. in the Staffhurst Wood area. This disposition held all summer; but with the autumn the troops went into billets, the village being occupied from October onwards by the Canadian Seaforth Highlanders, a crack Regiment from Vancouver B.C...During the winter Staffhurst Wood became the site of a very large munition dump, the whole wood being filled with stores of shells, etc. for the Coast defence. Our own contribution in this respect was the use of St Silvan's Church as a canteen for the large numbers of men of the R.A.O.C. and the Pioneer Corps working on the Dump...The military authorities fully appreciated the value of the canteen which was officially recognised by them for supplies from NAAFI.

"The Swan Picture Palace, the little cinema at the bottom of Hosey Hill, once the Swan Brewery's malthouse, remained open throughout the war and was well patronised by troops stationed in and around Westerham, airmen from Biggin Hill, Italian POW's and local girls who still have happy memories of this sudden influx of male escorts for the one-and-nine-pennies. But few took a chance with the 24 seats in the balcony upstairs where bats flew around and a notice warned you that you sat at your own risk."

"As we passed Sterling Engineering works next to the cinema at the bottom of the hill on our way to school 'up Hosey', we used to go 'one, two, three, HOP,' and on the 'HOP', try to get a look in through the half open windows. They'd blacked out the lower part, so the taller boys got a better view of the girls bending over their lathes."

Bob Combley whose father Jim Combley was maintenance engineer at Sterling during the war, describes the little factory that was set up in 1940 in what had been the old Phoenix Laundry at the bottom of Hosey Hill.

Before the war Sterling Engineering had been making gas stoves, mangles with wooden rollers and wringers with rubber rollers. But they were bombed out of London during the Blitz in 1940. Due to their pre-war products they had the skills and the equipment for machining iron castings and producing mechanical parts in many other metals. They were therefore able fairly easily to to turn these skills and equipment to making a wide range of war material. Hand grenades and 10lb Smoke Bombs were the two items that were produced in the greatest quantity during the war, possibly running to tens of thousands. Both the grenades and bombs came to the factory as rough castings and they were machined and fitted with all their working parts and finally coated with a treacley varnish before they were sent away to have their explosive filling put in.

In addition to the two items mentioned above, Sterling also made a range of small parts for use in radio and electrical equipment: brackets, turned parts and small insulated panels fitted with terminals and solder tags.

There could have been as many as 50 or 60 people working there, with an administration office up on Westerham Green between Mr Medhurst the tailor and Mills the baker.

Peter Finch
"Sterling Engineering also made Bangalore torpedos which were used during the landings on D-Day. These were large metal cylinders which were filled with explosive for blowing up barbed wire defences, and pushed into position with extension rods much like drain rods in principle. Whilst feeding these tubes into a machine George Wells who now lives in Granville Road, and who worked at the Sterling factory before his army call-up, got both hands caught in the works and the tops of all his ten fingers severed just above the quicks."

George Wells
"I was rushed up to Dr Hay's surgery where he sewed all ten tips back on again, and I have the scars to prove it to this day."

On the right-hand-side at the entrance to where Charlie Sharp's Garage used to be, (now Squerryes Mede), Bert Thorneycroft remembers a small depot for Lyons tea.

"Before the war I used to deliver tea all round the district for J. Lyons, the caterers, until my job came to an end with tea-rationing. In due course I went into the army and became a gunner. That small building was then taken over for the making of ball-bearings for Sterling Engineering. After the war the Westerham Press started in the building. Then a firm that made amphibious vehicles took it over and now it is Overload Electronics Ltd."

Geoff Hoath
"Mobile guns were positioned around the town, one being in a front bedroom at 26 High Street. Mrs Emily Hollands told the officer to go ahead with his firing as she and her husband would be in bed and the gunfire would not disturb them. The ground-floor front room had been shored up, the gun upstairs was packed around with sand-bag cushioning and the gun sticking out of a small cottage window was pointed towards Verralls' Corner."

Private vehicles commandeered to expand the mobility of the NFS (National Fire Service) were used for towing pumping appliances and taking stirrup pumps to 'incidents' at a time when large numbers of incendiary bombs set fire to barns, hay-stacks, hedges and fields around the parish and the service with its one and only fire-engine was severely stretched.

"The Oast House in the Croydon Road near the Fire Station became the Ambulance Station and ARP HQ where all 'incidents' were monitored. An 'incident' was the official name for a fire or damage caused by a bomb in any part of a Warden's district. Miss Kate Chatfield, who made her home with the Cosgrove family on the Green, was Westerham's full-time ambulance driver. Joan Bramwell, Mary Quirke and Kitty Papillon shared night-duties."

(In 1940), On Friday evening, Westerham spoke to the world on the wireless - and more particularly to British forces serving overseas - in a 20-minute programme, achieving well its ideal of presenting a picture of life at home to those far away places...Hosted by Wynford Vaughan-Thomas ... Mr Middleton[of gardening fame] introduced the programme in the quiet homely way which has become so famous. He told the world of Westerham's pride in General Wolfe and in Mr Churchill...and he paid a just tribute to the loveliness of the surroundings. During the programme it emerged that Westerham possessed more allotments than any other town in England of the same size.

"Market gardeners like us farmers were 'reserved occupation' people and George Bailey on Westerham Hill was the nearest to us. Then there was Hollingworth's and Jack Botley who also ran flourishing market gardens and supplied Westerham with fresh fruit and vegetables. Allotments and Botley's market garden covered a large area where to-day are Quebec Avenue and the King George's Playing Field. There were other allotments including one behind *Delagarde Farm* in the Croydon Road where is to-day's Fire Station."

30 September 1940. Hosey School records.

Considerable air fighting could be heard overhead and bombs were dropped. The boys took shelter under their desks.

Rosamund Winder (née Tyser)
"But air raid warnings didn't always come in time, and I remember having to pick Spitfire machine-gun 'links' from my baby Anne's pram in the garden at *Breaches*. Had there been time, I would of course have rushed the pram indoors and we'd have been down in the cellars. Those little pieces of metal linked the anti-aircraft shells and fell out of the sky during dog-fights over the town. We watched a number of planes being shot down, but it was sometimes almost impossible to tell whether they were theirs or ours, though on one occasion we did see five German planes come spiralling down."

Alan Mathews was nearly thrown by a huge bomb-crater in the middle of the A25, close to Verrall's Corner. He was cycling at about 5.0 am from his home, 45 London Road to his Post Office job in Oxted when an air raid warden in the High Street shouted out to warn him of the danger ahead.

Alan Mathews
"John Hooker who lived at number 91 High Street, was able to film the activity around this 'incident' using his cine-camera through his letter box to capture the ARP people and the police in action around the crater just outside his gate. As a 'reserved occupation' telephone engineer John was at home and couldn't resist fixing this scene on his door-step for all time, though he knew that it was illegal to do so. That bomb also removed some cottages on the curve across the road - next to where Jimmy English used to have his little cafe. There's a small piece of garden with a seat there now."

30 September 1940. WPC minutes:

...arising from the minutes, the matter of the Air Raid Shelter on the Green...it was requested that permanent lighting might be put in. The Chairman said that it should be attended by the Wardens. As regards notices, no doubt they would be posted in prominent places...and shelters are to be provided for the school children.
Concerning lamp standard in Quebec Square damaged by an army lorry. Cost of labour and replacement would be £10.
SRDC...not aware of the Council's war-time activities which they are authorised to delegate to Parish Councils.

Gardening: The Clerk reported on the cultivation competition for the tenants of the Currant Hill allotments. Only three had entered and the plots were so good that Cr Steven and Greenlees were giving a prize for each.

A complaint was made regarding the bomb crater on the Hosey footpath, now being dealt with.

Most men in the forces regarded those who had managed to escape the call-up with envy rather than indignation. At first, under the Schedule of Reserved Occupations issued in September 1939, men in a vast range of trades and professions were exempt from military service. But gradually one calling after another was removed from the list, or the age of reservation was raised. It was a fact that those who were required to remain behind usually had to work far harder than most men in the forces and on a more meagre diet...yet they continued to be seen as the lucky ones.

"We had two threshing machines going, the steam engine standing well back from the thresher and a long leather belt conveying the power from engine to thresher. Our Land Army girls picked things up as they went along. They weren't really trained, but mostly would tackle any job. We had a binder and sheaves that had to be stooked which they used to do, as well as any work with a hay fork. But they were useless if a rat was flushed out: they just stood and screamed!"

"Some of the Land Army girls got lodgings in and around Westerham and they also had a hostel on Marlpit Hill near Edenbridge. They were employed by the local farmers and they paid for their own accommodation out of their wages. Sometimes they came to us as part of a threshing gang. One hot sunny day they stripped down to their bras to get sun-tanned. We warned them not to because we were threshing barley which has little barbed hook things, but they wouldn't listen. They soon found out we were right. Next day they were in agony."

"They used to be moved around and there was a Miss Scott who lived with Arthur and Constance Dascombe, Constance being in charge of the Land Army girls. They mostly handled hay forks and hoes and not the heavy machinery. Miss Scott did secretarial work and a milk round for Jack Steven. We didn't get into the combine stage until late in the war and after. We had a small combine at *Force Green Farm* and grew a lot of grass seed. We didn't have much contact with *Squerryes Farm*."

Ethel 'Diamond' Charman (née Allen)
"I had to get one of the welfare ladies - it might have been Mrs Granville

Streatfeild - to help me when I had trouble with a Land Army girl. She was always late in at night, and gone again early in the morning but I knew she was bringing a man back though I never actually saw him. Anyhow, the Welfare people were very helpful and came and fetched her clothes from here one day, when she was away 'sick' at home."

Bob Wood

"There was a purpose-built NAAFI centre at Moorhouse where to-day is Redland Tiles. That catered for all the troops within a certain radius. We used to supply that NAAFI with potatoes and green stuff. We usually kept about 120 hens or more at Force Green, and each cottage kept about half a dozen or so for their own use. The foreman at the time was a Mr White and he and I had a pig between us. He lived in the cottage up above the barn. Of course we had to give up our meat ration, but we could get crushed barley and any pig-swill that was going. Actually, we kept two pigs as Mr Steven had one, and Bill White and I had the other one between us. When we'd killed the pigs we took them over to the butcher at Chipstead to cut them up for us."

In those days every butcher had his own slaughtering yard. At Woods, (later Church and now Larratt), right up until 1947, animals were herded from a cattle-truck parked outside the shop, down a ramp with sides to it, which was lowered to the pavement, up an alleyway between the butcher's shop and to-day's Churchill Gallery and into the slaughterhouse at the back. The doctors' surgery, now Churchill Gallery, was adjacent to the slaughterhouse where to-day Precision Engineer Peter Hasler makes aeronautical components for such advanced aircraft as the future *Eurobus*. Some stout hooks and a large wooden wheel with ropes in the roof are all that remains of the butchering that went on there over many years. 'Curly' Bell who was a meat grader for the Government throughout the war years did his slaughtering down in Quebec Yard behind Quebec Square, opposite the Old House at Home.

"People used to call it 'Workhouse Yard.' There were no back doors to those cottages then, and the toilets, like the slaughterhouse which belonged to Dove's, were down at the bottom of the garden. When we were kids we used to stop off there on our way home from school and watch them slaughtering a bullock, sheep or pig. Kids to-day don't have that sort of experience or interest. Later, when I (Bert Thorneycroft) worked there, we used to have to shoo them away sometimes, but they usually came back for another look. We used to bury bones, pig-skin and buckets of blood across the road in Jack Botley's nursery garden or give people the blood they asked for for their roses."

1 November 1940. Westerham's Infant School Records.

All the children were sent home at 3pm, as there had been no playtime, and a good deal of time had been spent in a cramped position under desks while there was aerial activity overhead.

"At school the little ones were told to remember to 'SAVE FUEL by snapping off Hitler's nose', which meant turning off the light switch."

27 December 1940. Westerham WI Archives. Maidstone.

Minutes:
Handicrafts: over 100 garments have been knitted for H.M. Forces.
Cookery: 1159 lbs. of jam have been made and 140 bottles and cans of fruit preserved.
Help has been given at local Canteen for evacuated school children.
A Waste Paper Depot has been run by members and 9 tons 12 cwts. of paper and cardboard have been collected and sorted.

Dr Hay and Dr Winder were asked to help out when a German plane crashed on the Common near Limpsfield Primary School. Such limited German as they had, as well as their medical skills were in demand on that occasion. But the two young airmen spat at them and warned them of imminent invasion by the Germans.

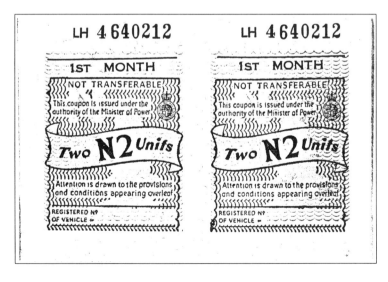

Motor fuel rations issued under the authority of the Minister of Power. In July 1941, clothes were also rationed joining food and petrol.

It was patriotic to be 'ill-dressed'

Even though we had the Canadians everywhere, and all sorts of people floating about - our place (*2 Deanery Road*) was never locked. People came and went and my mother used to put out the baker's money, the rent money, the fishmonger's and other money, all on the table on a Monday morning and everybody came in and helped themselves to what was theirs and nobody ever took anything or pilfered."

"In Crockham Hill we had Nurse Bishop from Four Elms, Dr Coulthard from Edenbridge and PC Ford (who wore black puttees) and lived at the Police House now called *The Old Laundry,* opposite what was in Victorian times the old Post Office, now called *Cobblers*, up the loop road on the right. The Victorian letter-box is still in the wall there. Mrs Scarlett and her daughter Miss Scarlett sold just about everything, where to-day still is a post office with antiques."

In Westerham Dr Hay managed his general practice single-handed from his home *Borde Hill* with help from Dr Beryl Hewett (née Furlong) who travelled three times a week from Penshurst and Dr Ellinor Carter Braine who came from Sevenoaks, so that the team was referred to affectionately as 'Dr Hay and the Girls'.

Dr Beryl Hewett (née Furlong)
"I left my car in Dr Hay's drive at *Borde Hill* and used his car and his petrol for domiciliary visits, and he did all the night calls and maternity work for the practice. We looked after the evacuated children at *Farley Croft* and at *Rusholme* in Crockham Hill. And though *Penicillin* had not yet arrived, we were able to treat patients with *Prontosyl* and *M & B 693* which were the earliest effective antibiotics."

Jean Hay
"Mary Quirke and Kate Chatfield drove my father Dr Hay on his rounds which saved him endless time. One day they parked over a bomb crater in Rysted Lane. A vigilant Air Raid Warden spotted it and made them move as there was an unexploded bomb underneath.
I used to answer the surgery phone at our home, Borde Hill. One day a call came from one of the Gordon Highlanders at that time stationed in Westerham. He began by listing a number of drinks they wanted to order for Christmas,

believing that he was through to the Brewery. I suggested that we did a good line in Castor Oil - which produced dead silence. Our phone number was only one digit different from the Brewery's. This confusion caused much amusement and resulted in an introduction of members of the regiment to Westerham folk who were invited to lessons in Scottish dancing at St Mary's Hall which proved very popular.

My father was driving down Titsey Hill one Sunday morning when out of the sky dropped an aircraft engine which just missed him. He got out, had a look round and found two dead Canadian fighter pilots and the wreckage of two planes scattered in all directions: they had collided in mid-air. Then my father noticed a man lying in the road with what remained of a bicycle on top of him. He had been hit by flying debris and was badly burned but made a complete recovery, after my father had managed to extricate him and drive him to hospital, and was later able to thank him in person."

"Westerham's District Nurse was Nurse Ford during the war, whose chief preoccupation (apart from her work) was trying to get home before the blackout and night raids began. She liked her patients to have their beds downstairs, close in under the stairs and up against a wall. 'Hurry up', she used to say to them. 'Don't waste time, it'll be soon be dark and the siren may go.' Westerham mothers-to-be did their best to oblige. But one mother at least had to manage without her: 'Nurse Ford just went home and left me to it', she said. 'But she came back after the All-Clear had gone.' Nevertheless, there are many who still remember Nurse Ford with gratitude and affection for her kindness, concern and care."

"From the Royal Oak down were the Royal Oak cottages, then there was the butcher Fred Baxter who also ran a taxi service during the war, and for some time after it. Of course he got extra petrol for that. Then there were two houses and the Wright's village shop which also did teas. But the little tea-room next to Wright's, kept by Mr and Mrs Stapley, was closed 'for the duration' as there were no longer young people in parties of week-end ramblers or hikers, or lads cycling out from London to enjoy the countryside."

The Rev. Oliver Fielding Clarke
The parish at this stage was lucky as regards bombing. Enemy planes were often over the place but only one cottage had been knocked about not long before I came. When the first big raid took place on London and much of the City was set on fire, we could see clearly the fierce light in the sky. Parish life went on as usual: there were still a number of evacuees, so that there were as many as 90 children in our church school, where in those pre-Butler Act days they remained till they were 14.
There were occasional 'incidents'. An evacuated nursery school was burned

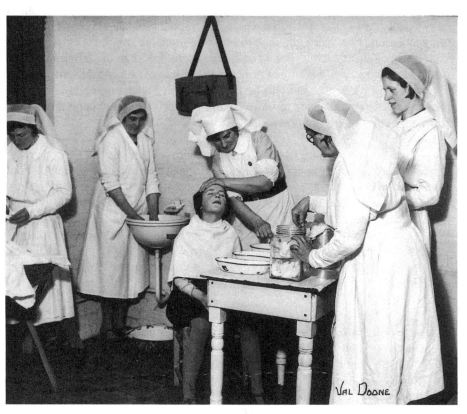

VAD nurses Dulcie Sharrad and Ruth Gadsby with Nurse Stevens, Trot Smith and Pat Gorick at the first aid post. The patient is a Miss Ford. Can any reader supply her Christian name?

down one night (at Acremead in Froghole Lane) *by a shower of incendiaries, when, fortunately, the entire school was in its air-raid shelter. But the London County Council, instead of taking this as a warning, moved the school into another big house a little over half a mile away. The result of this was an appalling tragedy of which I will say more later.*

With the experience of food rationing behind it, the public raised no objection to the coming of clothes rationing. Throughout the war, public opinion was always in favour of extending rationing as the best guarantee of fair shares. The clothes rationing was based on the points system also adopted by the Ministry of Food. For twelve months from 1 June, everyone was to receive sixty-six coupons, twenty-six of them in the form of the unused margarine coupons in the current book. Every item of clothing was given a coupon value, varying according to how much labour and material were needed to produce it. While clothes were at first provided on margarine coupons, fuel when it came to be rationed was to be supplied on clothing coupons until special ration books were ready. People over sixty-five would be able to exchange clothing coupons for extra fuel and the chilly North would get a 30 per cent larger ration than the sunnier South. Even dusters, handkerchiefs, face flannels and babies' nappies needed points.

"On Whit Sunday 1941, clothes rationing started. So, all the shops being closed, we were able to put up notices in our windows and pin the 'coupon value' tickets on individual garments. The Board of Trade made a point that we were to tell customers that clothes were being put on coupons not because supplies were scarce, but because they were too plentiful. The President, Oliver Lyttleton spoke on the wireless to appeal to the nation to remember that we would be being patriotic if we became 'ill-dressed'. It was to save factory space and by closing down clothing firms to release workers for the munition industries, he said. You had to part with coupons even for handkerchiefs or dusters and for babies' nappies. In those days there were four or five shops that were 'ladies and gentlemens' outfitters' in Westerham, not like it is to-day. Course, the next morning there was a sudden rush to buy, as everyone thought that coupon values would probably go up."

Margaret Payne
"As a child at the time, I remember that one quarter of a clothing coupon, folded diagonally and cut into four equalled a handkerchief. As a child too, when sweets came off rationing around 1950 and I asked at Woolworths for 6 ozs, I was disconcerted when they told me that they only sold them in ¼ lbs or ½ lbs. I who had always counted every single ounce of my precious sweet ration found that 6 ozs was as much as I could envisage."

FOOD FACTS

NEW *ways of using dried eggs*

They'll help you to give variety to your cooking

MOST women realize now what a boon it is to have eggs always at hand in a packet, and to be able to make delicious egg dishes often.

But not everyone realizes the large number of ways in which dried eggs can be used. Here are some suggestions for using them in ways which will be new to many women. Try them for yourself and see what variety you can get into your cooking with dried eggs.

If you haven't a sieve, get out the lumps from the egg powder by rubbing between the finger-tips.

Pastry looks better, tastes better, if you brush it over with a little reconstituted egg before baking.

To save fat in frying

Use reconstituted eggs for coating fish fillets, fish cakes, rissoles, bread, sliced cooked potato, before frying. You need less fat this way, as the egg forms a coating which stops the fat being absorbed.

A "fresh-flavour" tip for Scrambled Eggs

Have you tried adding a little mustard when making scrambled eggs? Add it with the other seasoning — half a teaspoonful of dry mustard for four eggs.

For "professional" pastry

Give your pastry the real professional touch by brushing it over with reconstituted egg before baking. The advantage of dried eggs is that you don't have to break a whole egg when you want to use a very small amount. You can reconstitute just the quantity you need for immediate use.

Better baking

Add dried eggs to scones, buns, dumplings, and pastry. It makes them richer, gives a better colour, as well as added nourishment. Use one to two level tablespoons of dried egg to half a pound of flour, mixing the egg powder dry with the flour.

Hard-boiled eggs

Reconstitute the eggs in the usual way, and pour into well-greased egg-cups or moulds — one egg to

Phil Johnson

"We moved to Crockham Hill in 1941 when my father's boss moved away from Greenwich. We went to *Little Court* where we lived in the cottage. Introduced to Hosey School, I found that foreigners were not welcome: ('Townies' on the run').

I remember a feeling of pessimism after the flush of London. It was very quiet and I couldn't accept the feelings of upper and lower class which existed. The school was very good, run on disciplined, almost military lines, but with far too much emphasis on sport instead of teaching. I didn't learn much that I remember and was posted to our printing press where we turned out all manner of publications, including forms for the K.E.C. These were handled very clandestinely, which I now realise was due to the unions."

Marjorie Thomson (née Johnson)

"The cottage was a shock, with pumped water, chemical toilets, oil lamps and kitchen range. It was the chauffeur's or gardener's cottage, now *Coachmans*. Our father was chauffeur-mechanic to a Mr Vesey whose timber firm Christie & Vesey in Greenwich was taken over by the Ministry of Supply. They dealt in timber for railway sleepers, telegraph poles, and Bailey bridges, jerricans and so on. They moved their office to *Little Court* in Crockham Hill and my father drove Mr Vesey up and down to Greenwich. I was 19 at the time and started by working at *Pilgrim House* for The Woolwich, cycling to and fro and in the snow, walking the five miles each way. Later I worked at *Little Court*.

Phil Johnson

"It had a magnificent view and soon became a way of life, although mother always a Londoner, never did accept it. Locals were guarded but very easy to befriend. We were situated in the fields between *Chartwell* and the village and *Chartwell* was being guarded by a Canadian regiment. At the Royal Oak Gracie and Bill Langridge blended a particularly potent brew of cider and the soldiers would regularly stumble along New Road, trying to get back on guard, but passing out and spending the night around us.

My first job was with Churchill's gardener Bert Hill, helping to pack a tea-chest of fresh fruit and vegetables for delivery to Mrs C. once or twice a week. He grew wonderful peaches, all of which he grew inside a muslin pouch and had to be picked and wrapped in tissue before packing. Roses had to be de-thorned and I recall Bert having a chastising letter from Mrs C. to the effect that she had found one that had been missed. I think that those boxes followed WSC all over the place.

One of the more memorable periods was working for Farmer Moore of *Froghole Farm,* under instruction from the Land Army girls. Exciting times. One year he took a chance and planted tomatoes everywhere - he must have

The 1914-18 war canon and shell cases which were removed from Westerham Green in the scrap metal drive.

known something because the crop was tremendous. Very few men on the farms then. There were balloon and gun sites in the fields around *Chartwell.* I remember these as very cosy little communities of gunners and WAAFS.

We didn't see much of aerial dog-fights in London but they were fairly commonplace still in Kent and were exciting viewing from the ground. We got to a wrecked plane that wasn't under guard, below Crockham Hill: a Dornier. We did have an ME 109 low across Hosey when we were in the playground. He let off a few rounds into the Common, only for show I think."

"Those Canadians thought pubs were selling apple juice. It clean bowled them over when they got their cider at the Royal Oak. When they got paid they used to stand us all drinks. Then we did the same for them...only some of us had our wives nagging at us to leave it alone and go home to help with putting up the black-out of a night-time, which took forever."

11 January 1941. WPC minutes:

The Gun: Ministry of Supplies.

Arrangements have been made for the removal and disposal of the gun. The cash received would either be paid to the Treasury or to any charity designated by the Council. The Clerk said he had consulted the Chairman who had suggested the local branch of the Red Cross Society. A cheque for £2 had been received and forwarded....

24 March 1941. WPC minutes:

The Green: Estimate to remove concrete blocks where the old gun stood, making good ground, and turfing that and other bare places £7 15s 6d.

Monica Capadose (née Bramwell)
"Right at the beginning of the war, when my family still lived at *Breaches,* my mother Joan Bramwell, her sister 'Millie' Sutherland, Kitty Papillon, Eileen Duggan and others ran a clothing exchange depot in the basement of *The Pheasantry.* The idea was to let the newly arrived evacuees have garments virtually for free. These exchanges were backed by local councils and staffed mainly by the WVS and were a great help in trying to meet the needs of growing children. I was about ten or eleven years old at the time and I remember helping out there. But one day I got it wrong, as I didn't know the difference between evacuees and some of the local residents and I charged an evacuee more than I should have done. In time the WVS took over the clothing of the evacuees - which I imagine was when they began their enormous WVS clothing depots. The enter-

prise at *The Pheasantry* probably only lasted for a matter of months...But then, so did the presence of most of the evacuees, for by Christmas 1939, the great drift homewards was well under way."

"Clothes could be handed in and were 'priced' at a certain number of coupons. Some other garment worth similar coupons could be taken in exchange. It worked wonderfully well. For many of us, new clothes were out of the question as the war went on, and anyhow, it was seen as being patriotic to be wearing well-worn clothes. Some mothers added different-coloured bands for lengthening growing childrens' clothes. Mind you, we did some funny things like painting our legs with burnt cork or cold tea and such-like and drawing a line down the back with an eyebrow pencil for the seam. Sometimes our legs ran with gravy browning if we got caught in the rain."

"MEND AND MAKE DO TO SAVE BUYING NEW the Government used to tell us over the wireless. I wonder we didn't go on with that after the war. Utility clothes were good'n all. They wore well, but you could always tell them. They did look skimpy somehow. No fullness anywhere."

25 July 1941. WPC minutes:

A special meeting of the Council in Committee and members of the Womens' Voluntary Service at St Mary's Hall, to consider the salvage and collection of rags, bones, bottles, tins, paper and old iron. The Chairman said that the Government had ceased to carry out this work and had delegated it to the Rural District Councils.
Suggestions were sought and put forward. Tradesmen to be asked to request customers to return bottles to them, and Crockham Hill to arrange similarly.

At Westerham Brewery, where Black Eagle Close now is, due to rationing of certain raw materials, from time to time there might be a shortage of Westerham Ales for delivery to local pubs. The Knight family of *Spring Ardens* occasionally took shelter in Reg Pike, the firm's cooper's shop or in the Brewery cellars. Head Brewer Peter Knight, in command of the local ARP and his next-door neighbour Sir John Dean, his deputy, of *Moretons* kept pigs in their adjoining gardens. Benefiting occasionally from a little spin-off from the brewery to bulk out their feed, they nevertheless remained sober for 'the duration'.

Peter Finch
"Some of my school friends went along to an army dump and came back with a case of hand grenade detonators about as thick as a pencil and some 20

feet of fuse-wire, used for priming hand grenades. As we were short of fireworks we used these to make bangers by lighting the end. We used to cut off bits of fuse wire and tuck them into the little bits of tube. They fizzed along and made bangs. We could also split fence posts with them."

"We had double-summer-time in the war. In Westerham, evensong was held in the afternoon because it wasn't possible to black out such a large building. We missed those railings down past the War Memorial when they were taken for the scrap metal drive. And we also missed the ringing of the Church bells which was stopped at the same time as they took away all our sign-posts and rounded up enemy aliens. And every household got a leaflet about what to do 'IF THE INVADER COMES'. We were told to stay put and avoid blocking the roads if the Germans did attack. Then we had another leaflet with more detailed advice on 'BEATING THE INVADER.'"

One German pilot who had to bale out during an air battle, ripped his parachute as he jumped but landed safely on a haystack beside the Sevenoaks to Westerham road. A passing bus stopped sharply, and the driver and conductor armed themselves with spanners before tackling the man. The pilot, thinking the couple were in military uniform, came to attention, gave a Nazi salute and said: 'Biggin Hill ist kaputt.' ('Biggin Hill is finished'). Bombs which had been meant for that airfield in one of the lunchtime raids had, in fact, fallen wide and destroyed only a line of telegraph poles. But the driver was so angry that he hit the pilot on the head with his heaviest spanner, knocking him out cold.

"Another luckless bale-out I saw was a German airman. A drove of Ju 88's were passing over in formation heading in the Croydon direction, when one plane was hit and broke into flames. The crew came out one by one and drifted away by parachute. But one chap either didn't have a parachute or it never opened. I watched him all the way down, and could see his arm and leg movements, then he screwed himself into a ball, I suppose to prepare for the impact. Although he was the enemy, I remember hoping his chute would open, and the strange feeling I experienced when I realised he wasn't going to make it. His body was found by French Canadian soldiers reported to be stationed at Limpsfield, but I would say *Clackets* would have been nearer the mark. I never did see what happened to the stricken Ju 88."

Bob Steven
"I recall an incident when the Battle of Britain was at its height. It was early Summer and I was working on a silo near the stables at *Force Green Farm.*
Overhead one of the many dog-fights developed between Spitfires and German planes. One Spitfire was shot down and crashed between my position

and Brasted. The pilot had baled out, quite high, towards Dunton Green and was parachuting gently down. Two German fighter planes then circled the parachute and very quickly set it alight, turning it from a mushroom shape to a descending pencil-like line. The pilot sped to his death followed by his parachute and a thin trail of smoke.

After the battle was over, two returning Spitfires flew low over where their comrade's plane had crashed and waggled their wings in respect."

"We were going to visit 'our pond' just on the edge of Big Wood one Sunday afternoon. At the last minute we deferred our visit to the evening, and at about the time we would have been in the vicinity, a V1 impacted and made a large crater, just about 100 yards north of *Buckham Thorns,* and about 50 yards from 'our pond'. I'm sure this one had our names on it, but it must have been that the Higher Authority was not quite ready for us."

Freda McBride (née Wright)
"I did the food returns for our shop in Crockham Hill as one of my war jobs. You cancelled in the ration books, with a pen or pencil, the regular rations: fats, sugar, tea, meat and bacon - as and when - for the week for which these had been allocated. You only cut out soap coupons or 'points'. Those were things that were not regular rations. Those you had to cut out, count, do up in bundles of 10 and send to the Food Office in Oakhill Road in Sevenoaks."

"When, about once a year, new ration books were issued, it was possible to change your retailer without explanation, but to do so in between was about as stressful as getting a divorce. You felt you could never go back to that shop again. It always paid to keep on good terms with your shopkeeper...you never knew when there might be 'something under the counter'. If you lost your ration book it was a serious matter. But you could get a replacement one at the Labour Exchange where the Wolfe Garage is to-day, on payment of a shilling, and on signature of a declaration witnessed by a responsible person."

Preparations against invasion were in hand throughout the country and continued to affect the lives of the population until at least 1942. One little pub-licised war measure was the distribution of reserve dumps of food in every town and village. The original German plan for invasion, later modified, involved seaborne assaults between Ramsgate and the Isle of Wight, supported by para-chute troops dropped behind Brighton and Folkestone and with follow-up land-ings between Weymouth and Lyme Regis. Invasion Committees arranged emer-gency slaughterhouses and bakeries and located enough wells to prevent a vil-lage going thirsty if the mains should be broken. Country vicarages were favour-ite store-places as were garages, farm barns and the garages and empty lofts.

The Rev. Oliver Fielding Clarke

I had not been in Crockham Hill very long before there arrived a formidable communication from some department in Whitehall on what to do if the enemy landed...With the help of the WVS and others a survey of our food supplies was therefore made...After this had been done food must be dumped in different parts of the parish, so placed that they could be reached without making use of the roads. These must be kept clear for troops moving to repel the invader...We soon got what we needed from the Ministry of Food, and I and my committee had an interesting and exciting time planning where our dumps would be...We soon had a scheme mapped out so that everyone throughout the scattered area could get food from one or other of the dumps without walking a yard on any road. Each dump was put in the charge of a responsible person in whose house or farm buildings the food was stored.

"In Westerham, emergency food was stored in a large purpose-built brick building put up just before the outbreak of war in Bloomfield Terrace. Nobody was supposed to know what exactly was stored there. After the war I heard that it was hundreds of tins of corned beef, biscuits, soup, condensed milk, margarine and tea. In case of incendiaries or a fire, an emergency Static Water Tank was set up alongside it in which local children had a fine time playing and splashing about. There were also stores of food (ships' biscuits etc.) in lock-ups at Charlie Sharp's Garage and a major ARP Stores Depot at Dunbrik. Galvanised iron and asbestos sheeting, tarpaulins, timber and other materials were stored there as well as ladders and buckets for the protection of, and first aid repair work to bomb-damaged buildings. Dunbrik just beyond Sundridge is still to-day a Council depot."

George Brown

"I used to work for Bond's Garage at The Mill in Brasted where Johnson's builders' yard now is. But the Army took us over. So we all had to find other jobs and I went to work for the Council on their ARP vehicles, ambulances, rescue vehicles and so on at their Dunbrik Depot. Like people did in Westerham, we had two or three RAF lads billeted with us at various times at *10 Alms Row*. They were working on aircraft recovery at *Combe Bank* in that field where there is the little old aerodrome, just inside the lodge there, near where to-day is *Sundridge Rectory*. The large field on the right-hand-side of Combe Bank Drive off Chevening Road was stacked high with crashed aircraft for breaking up."

After the war Sir William Rook settled to live at *Northfield* in Crockham Hill. He was knighted in 1941 for his services to the nation in two World Wars and as Director of Sugar during WW2, had controlled sugar rationing throughout Britain.

118

6 October 1941. WPC minutes:

SRDC wrote quoting information given in a recent Ministry of Home Security Circular. A high explosive bomb in a certain place had caused energizing of the street lighting circuit, resulting in the lamps (which had not been removed) being lit up. Precautions should be taken to prevent this happening. The Clerk said he had replied to the effect that all lamps and switches were removed, and cables sealed immediately on the outbreak of war.

The SRDC requested the assistance of the Parish Council in the matter of the collection of iron and steel railings for use as scrap. Each member promised to look round his or her own area and send in a list by the end of the week.

And they surely must have done just that. For railings are missing from all around the town to this day, amongst which are those which once flanked the path leading down past the War Memorial in Westerham Churchyard, railings around a number of family vaults and the First World War shell-case posts and chain railings that used to surround General Wolfe's statue on the Green. In a number of places such as outside *St Helena's /Prospect House* on the corner of New Street with the High Street it is still possible to detect the darkened metal stumps in brick and stone walls where railings were cut down by acetylene torches. Just one short run of substantial residual iron railings remains in Westerham Churchyard to-day - where there is a sign saying PUBLIC FOOTPATH AND CAR PARKS.

The churchyard railings which were removed in the scrap metal drive.

June Smith (née Jenner)

"I well remember the day the lorry came and took all the railings away from the fronts of Chestnut Villas on the right-hand-side at the top of Madan Road, opposite the new Police houses. Miss Perry used to have a sweet shop in one of those houses. And railings disappeared too along London Road in front of the *Grange Cottages* where Len Waterhouse lives to-day and in the churchyard. Family vaults lost their iron railings, amongst these being the vault of the Hansard family who had built and lived at *Darenth Towers.*"

As for that old First World War German cannon behind General Wolfe's statue on the Green - Mollie Cosgrove, Fred Cull, Mons Bell, June Jenner, 'Brownie,' Alan Matthews and surely many others who grew up in Westerham between the two World Wars remember climbing on it, using its wheels to reach the top and peer down into its gun-barrel "filled with fag-ends and sweet-papers."

Mons Bell

"On my way home from Sunday School one day, I had just cleared the top of the gun when I caught and tore a pocket of my brand new suit as I slid down the other side. My mother was not best pleased when I got home."

Along with many others, Mary Kenward (née Petty) and June Smith (née Jenner) have,

"happy memories of school parties when we collected bushels of rose hips from the hedgerows around *Force Green Farm.*"

13 October 1941. Westerham Infant School Records.

Four girls were sent at 3.15pm to take to the WVS collector, 74lb of rosehips collected by the children for jelly-making under the Government scheme.

8 November 1941. WPC minutes:

The Council held a Special Meeting at Brunswick House. The business was that of a secret character. The Sevenoaks Rural District Council notified this Council that Westerham has been declared a Nodal Point, Category B, by the competent authorities. They had been directed by the Regional Commissioner to make application to this Council, as Trustees of the Green, for permission to erect a steel dam on the Green - to provide a static water supply for fire-fighting purposes.

After some discussion the proposal was approved, provided the Green will be made good to this Council's satisfaction when the necessity for the water supply has been removed. It was agreed that the District Council be asked if they have considered the danger that might arise should the dam burst and cause flooding of Vicarage Hill and Quebec Square, this Council being of the opinion that a better site would be on The Grange Estate.

19 December 1941. Hosey School Records.

The usual Xmas Dinner at noon was shorn of much of its glitter; no nuts, no sweets, no crackers, etc. yet as jolly as ever.

22 December 1941. Westerham WI Archives. Maidstone.

W.I. Fruit Preservation Depot:
401 lbs of Jam, 29 bottles of fruit and 12lbs chutney.
Hall lent to soldiers on Sundays for Religious Services.
Hall lent as sleeping accommodation to passing troops.
Knitting for Merchant Navy Comforts Service.

Bob Wood
"When field drainage was being put in all around *Force Green Farm*, in about 1942, the Kent Agricultural Committee employed German and Italian prisoners of war."

"Meals in restaurants were not rationed, but it became illegal to serve more than one main course at any meal. Cutlery got so short that some cafes chained their spoons to stop them being 'liberated', and in June 1942 a five-shilling maximum was introduced."

To bridge the gap between rations and appetites the government expected every family to eat out, on average, about one day a month and for some members of the family to have their main meals at school or work. School dinners, which before the war had been available only to 250,000 children, were by its end almost universal. Factory canteens had numbered 1,500 in 1939. By 1945 there were 18,500 and any firm over a certain size was legally compelled to provide one. The most important of all was the British Restaurant, a simply furnished cafeteria, providing a filling meal very cheaply. Provided on a non-profit-making basis by local authorities they were guaranteed against loss by the government.

20 April 1942. WPC minutes:

Rural Workers: National Union of Agricultural Workers Local Branch...Reminder of hardship endured by the present food rationing, which falls heavier on the Rural Workers than those where canteens are in use. Can relief be given by setting up a communal feeding centre?
The Clerk said he had replied stating that a British Restaurant is being fitted up and opened by the SRDC at an early date.

"It opened on Monday 5 October 1942 with the kitchen on the ground floor and the restaurant upstairs, between which, a perilous lift worked by ropes which became ever greasier and more slippery, food was transported. One unforgettable day the lift tipped a full load down the shaft. Prime movers were Violet Wells, Mrs Ralph, Joan Bramwell, Millie Sutherland, Ann Hetherington, Jean Sellers, Mrs Draper and Mrs Moss (who later cooked at the King's Arms)."

Joy Lee (née Sutherland)
"My grandmother, General Currie's wife used to heat her dishes in the oven, wrap them in a white cloth in a basket and with her little Cairn in tow, sally forth from *Monksway* to the British Restaurant in the London Road. For 1s6d per head, she got two very good courses which she had not had to cook, nor had she had to make inroads on her meat and other rations. This excellent service was from Mondays to Fridays and you could eat upstairs in the restaurant for the same price. It was a wonderful service which was a Godsend to many."

With the outbreak of war and food rationing, at Hosey School the numbers of boys taking hot meals increased to 140, necessitating new arrangements. Major Warde gave a piece of Common Land for the erection of a new canteen with a dining-room, together with a small strip of land for use as a school garden.

Air Raid Shelter: As the result of a meeting between the Allotments Managers and the Emergency Committee of the SRDC, the position of the suggested shelter was in accordance with military requirements. If the Parish Council refused to agree, they would be responsible for any serious consequences.

Currant Hill: the Clerk submitted an agreement the Council had made with Sir Henry Pelham regarding the use of part of his land as allotments for the period of hostilities.

Ethel 'Diamond' Charman (née Allen)

"My husband had an allotment at Currant Hill where he built sties and kept several pigs, chickens and rabbits, as well as growing masses of vegetables. He never sold anything that we could eat."

Peter Finch

"There was an occasion when the siren didn't go, because apparently a squadron of FW 190's came in below the radar, hugging the ground right the way across, heading for London. I was out in the yard at Charlie Sharp's. As youngsters we were all trained to spot aircraft using charts of silhouette outlines, so I knew what they were. They were flying so low you could see the pilots and the crosses on the sides of the planes. I remember running up the yard and climbing the structure near the grease-bay to get closer to them. There were one or two squadrons of these FW 190's flying absolutely level and just above the chimney pots. They loosed off some rounds from their machine-guns and I believe they fired at Westerham Station. Then the whole lot of them lifted up and cleared Westerham Hill and carried on, so I heard, to bomb the Admiralty.

Captain Cooper who lived at *Horn's Hill Lodge* worked at the Admiralty: I believe he may have been deputy Judge Advocate of the Fleet, anyhow he worked at the Admiralty, and we looked after his great big Humber Snipe. Believe it or not, in that bombing of the Admiralty, that car got damaged. I remember that the next day, Charlie Sharp and somebody else went up and brought it back, full of holes. I've never forgotten those Fokker-Wulfs. It was all over in a matter of a few seconds: and I remember feeling no fear at their being so close. Captain Cooper was instrumental in helping to get a number of chaps into the Navy by taking up individual cases when local men were called up, if they were mad keen to join the Royal Navy. You just went along and talked to Captain Cooper."

Peter Finch

"I went fishing with a chap who was a couple of years older than I was and who could always lead me astray. He told me we were going to go fishing in *Chartwell* lake that week-end. I said we wouldn't be able to get in: but of course he knew better. So we cycled to Horns Hill, left our bikes at the top by *Northfield* and with our fishing rods on our shoulders set off down the valley towards the lake. But suddenly, a voice called out: HALT! DON'T MOVE! And troops armed with rifles appeared from the woods all around as if from nowhere and surrounded us. We told the officer we were just going fishing. We'd thought that with the war on, and nobody there...But apparently with our rods on our shoulders we'd looked like men armed with rifles. He gave us a good telling off and threatened us with the guard room, and if we were ever seen up there again...we'd probably be shot on sight."

14 November 1942. WPC minutes:

Cr E. J. Hollingworth commented on the dangers of children climbing on to the seat, by the fencing round the dam, and leaning over. The local section of the National Fire Service to be asked to move the seat to a site approved by the Council; and to improve the appearance of the dam by clearing weeds and grass.

30 November 1942. WPC minutes:

The business was to consider a letter received from the Royal Academy of Arts. The Secretary wrote:

'The President of Council of the Royal Academy requests me to enquire whether the Parish Council of Westerham would accept from the Royal Academy, for permanent possession by Westerham in some public room, a replica in bronze of the portrait head of the Prime Minister by Sir William Reid Dick KCVO, RA., which was lately presented to Mr Churchill by the Royal Academy.

When the suggestion of this gift was made to Mr Churchill, he fully approved it. The only condition attaching to the gift is that it should be in some public building'. It was unanimously agreed that the offer be accepted. As regards the public building the following three were considered:-

(1) The Library St Mary's Hall, for the present, with the proviso that should a Public (County) Library or Council Chambers be erected at a subsequent date the replica would be placed there.
(2) The present County Library was not suitable.
(3) Quebec House. Would be good but belongs to the National Trust and applies to General Wolfe.

It was decided that the Library St Mary's Hall be selected ...and that the trustees of St Mary's Hall be written to asking for permission to place the replica in the Library, the Council bearing all expenses.

The replica bust was unveiled on 5 February 1944 and is now in the Council Chamber of Westerham Parish Council at Russell House, Westerham.

Leading up to 'Operation Overlord'

EPRIVED of sweet things, we used to pester the lives out of those Canadians and jam became one of our few luxuries. School children, Brownies and Cubs were encouraged and sometimes even press-ganged into combing the hedgerows for berries of all kinds. To foster this good housekeeping, in 1943 the Ministry of Food augmented the sugar ration by issuing an extra two pounds of sugar at harvest time. There were two recommended strengths of jam: 'weak', which was made with little sugar, was 'runny' and had to be eaten within about two months before it went mouldy, and the real stuff that lasted as long as greed would allow. The WI were heavily into jam-making in bulk and official jam-making centres were set up where the jars had to be properly labelled giving the date and place where the jam had been made and at which 'boil'. According to their records, Crockham Hill turned a bumper crop of plums into jam that year."

Doris Daigle (née Westfold)
"I was 25 when in January 1943 I married a 28-year-old Canadian from a little village called Rogersville, who had come over with the First Division of Canadians. We met at the Beadles Lane Gospel Hall Chapel in Old Oxted where every evening, troops were offered cups of tea or coffee and biscuits instead of the alternative, a drink at one of the four pubs locally. He was billeted at *Swallowfield* on Limpsfield Common and despite the difficulty of both of us having to arrange to synchronise our 48-hour leaves to meet and get to know each other better, we were eventually married. I had borrowed a dress from a friend because of the coupon situation, but as Jack had omitted to bring along his official Canadian document, we had to do things all the wrong way round with a short service at the Chapel and a reception back at my home until on the Tuesday we were legally married, Jack wearing his Royal Canadian Engineers uniform and I my WAAF uniform.

We were only to have a few 48-hours' leaves together before he was posted overseas and in July 1943 sailed for Sicily where on landing, he was mortally wounded. He is buried in the beautiful Canadian War Cemetery at Agira in Sicily, along with 483 other Canadians.

My mother and one of my sisters travelled to Compton Bassett where I was stationed at that time, to break the news of his death to me. After the war, in 1947 the Canadian Government's Free Passage Scheme enabled me, along with many other bearers of the Canadian Government Passes offered to wives, widows and children of members of the Canadian Forces Overseas, to visit my late husband's family. I sailed in the *Aquitania* taking six days to reach Halifax, and then went on to New Brunswick. It wasn't easy, fairly traumatic, without my husband as the link, but they couldn't have been nicer to me for the year that I was over there."

At 4 am in the dark hours of Monday 18 January 1943, 40 enemy bombers crossed the Channel, while a covering attack by 10 aircraft came in from the east. Scrambled instantly from West Malling, aircraft of 29 Squadron challenged the raiders over the Weald of Kent. In the engagement a Dornier 217 was shot down over Westerham by Wing Commander C.M. Wight-Boycott and his radar operator Flying Officer A.M. Sanders in a Beaufighter. There were no survivors.

"The pilot of an RAF plane shot down near to us came knocking on our door to reassure himself that we had not been hurt, when despite making valiant efforts not to fall on to us, he ended up crashing close by."

"There was a plane shot down in the dark about four o'clock in the morning up behind *Pilgrim House*. The buzz soon went round if anything dropped, passed round by the emergency service I suppose, when the fire-engine came back. You made enquiries and someone always seemed to know. I was just a young school-boy and I knew where to go so I shot straight up there on my bike. It was just a scene of devastation all through the undergrowth. A great swathe cut where it had hit the ground and there wasn't so much as a thing one could recognise as part of a plane."

Bob Wood
"The field below that crashed plane was absolutely covered with incendiaries which must have been its cargo for dropping over Biggin Hill or London. They usually fell in a cluster, often from *Molotov Breadbaskets* or *Cocktails* which split open in the air, scattering a hundred or more bombs over an area. Ordinary incendiary bombs were about a foot long by two inches in diameter, weighed about two pounds and were quite easy to bury or put out, so long as they hadn't already started a fire."

"We were able to rifle their pockets and find bars of very dark chocolate with German wrapping and writing on them. There was the trunk of a person with one arm and there was a gold ring. I just couldn't leave that there. Someone was going to have it so it might as well be me, but it took a lot of getting off. I had to use my army jack-knife to amputate his finger. Even now I can see it lying there on the twisted metal. I've still got that ring though my mother and father

126

told me off when I got home and said it would haunt me for the rest of my life. The lad who was with me is dead now. There's a name engraved around the inside. I've been tempted to write to someone like the people at the Imperial War Graves Commission or the Imperial War Museum to let them know I've got the ring so that the family would know that I'd return it to them...But might I even to-day be in trouble for having taken it? Somehow I've never wanted to risk telling anyone official like that about it."

John Warde
"At some time in the eighties, the Army arrived to dig that plane out of the North Downs. It was thought that there might be live bombs still on board. It turned out to have been a reconnaissance plane with some primitive radar system and the two pistons were taken to Biggin Hill."

George Collins of *Force Green Farm* was out rabbiting shortly after that, close to where the plane had crashed.

"I lost my ferrets below ground there, so went to get a spade to dig them out, and as I did so, I dug up a Sterling silver swastika brooch. Its about 3/4" square with some of the paste jewels still on its face and a safety-pin fitting in working order at the back."

Phil and Ernie Fleet (of *Force Green Farm*)
"When they dug that plane out they found the pilot still sitting there. So they put him back in, just buried him where he was."

Fred Cull, an old HOBA Scout, who has been in the fighting in North Africa from the beginning of the campaign, (in 1943) *sent us a subscription of ten shillings 'as a token of appreciation of all the useful things Scouting taught him while he was in the Troop'. Thank you Fred, wherever you may be.*

In connection with that campaign in the Middle East, at St Mary's Church Westerham, the church bells, silent against the possibility of the invasion they would announce, were rung with joy for the Alamein victory in 1943.

15 March 1943. PC minutes:

Parochial Church Council Complaints:
Need for Public Convenience:

Complaints of committings of nuisances by persons in parts of St Mary's Churchyard during the hours of darkness. Such matters had assumed most ob-

jectionable proportions. Cr Bennett stated that such happenings were prevalent in other parts of the town, and it was considered that provision should be made for men. At present there were no places available and suggested the Old Fire Station (where is to-day's post office car park) *...the absence of a public convenience, and prevailing conditions were a disgrace to any town or village.*
The whole matter to be submitted to the Public Health Committee of the Sevenoaks Rural District Council.

"Even local postmen couldn't go into Staffhurst Wood which was used as a vast ammunition dump, without producing their identity cards - and this also applied to The Royal Oak. There were NO SMOKING signs everywhere and ammunition for the dump from railway goods yards reached Staffhurst Wood via the 'Top Station' at Edenbridge."

David Hill (Ranger for East Surrey Open Spaces)
"To make an example of them and to deter any potential spies, two small boys found trespassing within the perimeter of the camp were smartly bundled into the back of a military truck, blindfolded and dumped a short distance away. In the spring, there would have been wild wood anemones and bluebells all through those woods. A few good quality roads, made from the thousands of tons of *Blitz* rubble transported from London as hard core foundation with a tarmac surface, and a large reinforced concrete drinking water tank some 5feet high and 25 feet in diameter survive to this day. There are several of these tanks in the area and all are thought to have had a metal lining. Sand-bag topped trenches, then 6 feet deep, for the troops in air raids are still just discernible and a few well-grown trees to-day sprout strands of barbed wire once attached to striplings, which 50 and more years later, are now deeply embedded within substantial trunks.

There was a miniature railway network criss-crossing the whole area for moving around the stacks of bombs, shells and every kind of ammunition, buried in shallow pits and trenches. Static water tanks were positioned at intervals in case of fire, and local people felt distinctly uneasy about such a dangerous collection in their vicinity with incendiary and other bombs raining down.

In 1944 a VI destroyed a large house called *The Horns*. The troops had just gone off for coffee at the Silvan Church at 11.00 that Sunday morning when a Spitfire caught up with the thing as it trundled on its way to London and tipped it with its wing, sending it crashing down on to the house which was totally demolished. In the Staffhurst Wood area a Dornier crashed close to Colonel Webber's *Gincox Farm* and a 109 near *High Ridge Farm*."

Bob Wood
"When the whole lot vanished overnight along with the troops for D-Day, everyone breathed a sigh of relief. After the war, Jack Steven bought a dozen of

the large static water tanks that had been deployed around Staffhurst Wood munitions depot. He brought them back to *Force Green Farm* where they made splendid storage units for corn."

Freda McBride (née Wright)
"I used to ride my bike through Staffhurst Wood and they never stopped me. I always went everywhere on my bike so I just carried on - and they let me. All the stores of ammunition were separated off with paths in between. Stacks were separated by gaps - and they didn't pile it too high. There were ammunition depots all over Groombridge too at that time."

Malcolm Taylor
"At Hosey School one day two Messerschmitts came over us, passing by our tall classroom windows at tree-top level and going on to machine-gun their way up Madan Road heading towards Westerham Hill. They flew so low that poor David Wells' wife had gun-shot through her apron which just didn't injure her, and the Westerham Laundry van travelling along Pilgrims' Way was peppered with bullets the length of one side. A pilot bailed out over Brasted* and came down just close to the church. His plane was on fire and I remember seeing the poor man whose parachute was also in flames fall to the ground where he died."

Anthony Kallend
"At *Deepdale* on Westerham Hill, a fine beech tree which was badly damaged in the hurricane of 16 October 1987, was felled in 1994. Cut into logs, a number of bullets, no doubt dating from the enormous military activity around Biggin Hill during WW2, were found in various places. All the bullets are to-day deeply embedded in the wood which by 1994 has grown out around them."

"Every now and again there were white painted numbers in white painted circles down the central white lines. Drivers had to follow their own number by the feeble light from dimmed headlamps as they didn't know where they were supposed to be going and there were no road signs anyhow."

Audrey Cowell (née Ricketts, then Mrs Frank Taylor
and subsequently Mrs Richard Cowell))
"On 30 March 1944 my husband Frank Taylor's destroyer *HMS Laforey* was torpedoed and sunk by a German U-boat off Salerno in the Bay of Naples. By that time we had moved from French Street Westerham up to Tatsfield, to a cottage on Ricketts Hill that we were put in touch with by Miss Deane, and which was rented for us by the Admiralty. We had two children then and our third, whom my husband was never to see, was born at Tatsfield. All four of us used to spend the nights on the floor in our Morrison shelter which was a sort of

large dog's kennel with wire all around us like a cage. We had a barrage balloon outside our front gate and the Canadian balloon crew used to give my little ones jam tarts."

"There were all sorts of troops. The Liverpool Kings, a rough old crowd but a jolly good lot. They had a marvellous band for dances at St Mary's Hall. At all of them we had the bands of whichever troops were here. *The Pheasantry* was commandeered. *The Breaches, Winterton House, Oak Lodge,* and a number of big houses up on Farley Common like Mrs Rook's *Farlowe* and *Squerryes Court.* They were all full of troops or officers, and as one lot left, others took their place."

Amongst units living under canvas or billeted in large houses and many smaller homes in the area around Westerham and towards Edenbridge were women of the ATS transport and artillery sections, men of the RAF Regiment, the Royal West Kents, the Welsh Guards, the RASC, the Pioneer Corps, the Military Police, the Royal Engineers, the Royal Artillery, the London Scottish and the Royal Sussex. And from Canada to these distant parts came the Princess Patricia's Canadian Light Infantry, the Edmonton Regiment of Canada and the RCAMC - taking back with them as their war-brides, a number of local girls who still live in Canada.

"No extra coupons were allowed for wedding dresses, but my sister, who was a Wren, was able to choose and borrow one of Eleanor Roosevelt's nine wedding gowns presented to the WRNS by the British War Relief Society of the USA. She was married in Westerham Church, had a nine carat 'utility' ring from Fuller's the Jewellers, (30s 9d in 1943) and was driven to and from the church by her brother-in-law, using some of his 'Agricultural Petrol'. That ring has lasted fine. But the wedding-cake wasn't up to much. Mum did her best and had been saving the ingredients for weeks, but the use of icing sugar for cakes was prohibited so she just put a 'V' for victory in silver balls on the top. They both had forty-eight-hour passes and spent the precious time together sitting on the front 'somewhere in England' surrounded by rolls of barbed wire."

Don Adams
"I remember a Spitfire crashing close to the T-junction at the top of Goodley Stock, about 100 yards along on the left on the way down into Crockham Hill. We'd been watching the dog-fight going on overhead and bits falling off one of our planes, and we saw it crash, so we hurried along to see what we could do. The poor lad was lying there dead in a tangle of metal. Officers came from Biggin Hill to inspect the crashed plane which they soon dismissed as valueless, not worth salvaging, just 'scrap'. We were disgusted by their callous attitude towards that young pilot we'd just been watching squirming about in the sky.

Later on, a truck came and collected the body, but it was as if the possible recovery of the plane was of more importance, and clearly that one, like its young dead pilot was of no interest to them."

19 April 1943. WPC minutes:

Dig for Victory Campaign: copies of leaflets prepared by the Ministry of Agriculture and Fisheries for distribution...allotment holders had taken them when paying their rent.
It is considered that the convenience is required at once, and the Old Fire Station could be utilised and is available. It could be converted into a temporary convenience immediately.

"A Hurricane and a Spitfire both crashed at Marlpit Hill and a German Dornier bomber at Bardogs Farm at Toys Hill. We picked up one German. The chap had come down on his 'chute', landing in a cabbage field alongside what to-day is Crockham Hill's War Memorial Sports Ground. He was lying there on the ground and we knew what we'd got to do. So we all stood over him with our rifles trained on him but shaking with fear. If he'd suddenly dived for a gun it would have been different. He only had some grazes so we dragged him out to the main road and the military came and picked him up. They'd crashed somewhere over Merle Common way and the rest of the crew were all killed."

21 May 1943. WPC minutes:

Public Rights of Way: record should be made of public rights of way which have been or may be ploughed up for corn production in order to prevent such rights being lost to the public.

12 July 1943. WPC minutes:

Public Conveniences: the scheme for the provision of a public convenience at the George and Dragon Hotel is to proceed on the basis that any capital money expended by that (SRDC) Council on structural alterations will be repaid by the owners at the termination of the agreement. In the end it was agreed that the matter be deferred until after the war...

In the event, the owners of the property, (the parents of Bill Thomas in the London Road), understandably would not agree to the terms, and so the matter rumbled on, cropping up at almost every Parish Council meeting until well after the war was over when one was built in Fuller's Hill.

"As the war dragged on, Prisoners of War, with POW on arm-bands became a familiar sight and were a useful force on the farms. They didn't seem to bother anyone and I should think they were jolly glad to be here. We had them when we were potato-picking and very decent chaps they were and no trouble to anyone. They came to work every day either from a camp at Tonbridge or another one along the A25, up the Rips on the way from Westerham to Oxted."

Redland PLC
Some of the POWs worked for Moorhouse Brick Tile and Concrete Products Ltd set up around 1935 by managing director Captain Bernard Thorpe (whose name lives on through the well known local estate agency group he also founded, now called Debenham & Thorpe.) Tile manufacture was suspended during the war but Ron Wells, works manager with RedlandTiles (which took over the business in 1946) recalled production getting under way after the war.

We started off with four or five British chaps; the rest were all prisoners of war. As time went on, gradually more men were demobilized, and others who had been comfortably off at some occupation, labelled 'reserved', found themselves looking for a job. I am not sure which I preferred - prisoners or the mixed bag we finished up with - Canadians, ex-jail birds, and any nationality you'd care to mention. I remember well that on many Monday mornings the machine couldn't run until the local magistrate had held court and discharged enough men so they could come to work.

Richard Thorpe
"Since during the war years there would be virtually no building requiring tiles, and in any case the younger members of the staff were being called up, in 1939 my father Bernard Thorpe closed down his works at Moorhouse 'for the duration', leaving the padlocked premises to be patrolled by security watchmen."

Richard and Doreen Abbott
"Our father Tom Abbott was head gamekeeper for the Leveson-Gower family of *Titsey Place* and throughout the war years we lived in the *Keepers Cottage* alongside the Moorhouse works. In time the NAAFI supply depot at Moorhouse packed up and an ordnance depot for the repair of military vehicles took its place. A Major Mitchell was in command at the POW camp, Captain Tolhurst, his second in command being billeted with us. Our father, one of whose jobs was the rearing of pheasants for the Leveson-Gowers, was forever having to remove wire snares, etc set by the prisoners in the woods and hedgerows around *Broomlands Farm* where rabbits from the adjacent sand-pit also abounded. And the German POWs awaiting repatriation, who used to chase his ducks from the pond close to the brickworks, were penalised by being denied privileges for

trying to bag them for their pot."

Peter Steven
"We had Italian POWs digging ditches out for us at *Squerryes Home Farm.*
They used to cook their chips in oil in old petrol cans out in the field and they
made little aeroplanes out of silver coins like florins, and then gave them back to
you. Various officers and troops were in the *Court* and in the estate buildings at
the back, the old stables and the grooms' accommodation. We were driven nearly
mad when the REMEs who had mobile workshops just over the fence by our
kitchen window started up at 7.0 in the morning. There was a searchlight, a
listening device and a pair of Browning machine-guns in a field below *Garden
Cottage* up the lane opposite us, just past the oast house. My sisters were older
than I was and attracted the attention of the local soldiery, so that they sometimes
visited us. One of them whilst cleaning his rifle in what we called 'the den' blew
a hole in the wall."

"The 'Eyeties' used to sing Italian opera while they worked and they just
loved any of us kids going near them. They gave us their army badges, showed
us how to make a hooting noise by blowing on blades of grass stretched over our
fingers and made pencil-boxes for us out of detonators. They knew all the different kinds of grasses. The ones that were good for picking your teeth. The ones
that made good whistles, or darts, and some for looping into nooses which, when
pulled tight, catapulted the heads of the grasses like miniature cannon-balls."

"I don't know how those Italian POWs were free to do so, but their guards
always seemed very relaxed about them, and I remember them going from house
to house on Limpsfield Chart, trying to sell the whistles they shaped from wood
they had got locally. They made quite a sweet sound when you blew into them
and they also sold charm bracelets that they made out of old jerricans."

May Tidy (née Taylor)
"I worked for a short while selling tickets at the Swan Picture Palace and
the Italian POWs had a coin which was very similar to our shilling which they
tried to pass off. If I didn't spot them, the money was docked from my
earnings...and I was doing that little evening job after work, to save enough for
a new bike. I was with the solicitors Wheeler Brill & John at Oxted at the time
and cycled through the blackout from my home on Limpsfield Chart and back
again, and to the Swan in the evenings. The troops used to wash their army
trucks in Whitemare Pond, which has been filled in since then, beside the
Limpsfield Chart Cricket Ground. Our parents told us school-age children we
were not to speak to any of those Canadian soldiers, but we watched the ones
from *Cronklands* playing football on the Cricket Ground and enjoyed hearing

the Princess Patricias playing their bag-pipes. Two of those Canadians occasionally gave my grandmother some eggs and bacon when she dropped a little basket to them out of the window. Sadly we heard later that both of them had been killed in France."

Diana McCurrich (née Passmore)
"We lived at *Ridlands* on Limpsfield Chart and I remember as a child of about six, waving to the Canadians in the military camp across the road and their waving back. Later the camp was occupied by Italian or German POWs. At that age, any foreigner was just a 'foreigner' to me."

"My sister brought a Pole home, but when she brought a German POW to tea, my father insisted on walking him back to the camp afterwards to make sure he got back alright. But they didn't seem to keep much of a check on them. He was a very nice young man."

Malcolm Taylor
"A huge unexploded bomb fell where Hartley Road is to-day, and when they decided to explode it, my mother (Daisy Taylor) was taken by ambulance with her three-day-old baby Joy, to the Long Pond along the A25 while this was done."

Ernest Bevin's one really unpopular decision was the 'grannies' call-up', the registration for war-work, in July 1943, of women aged from 46 - 50. This proved to be the first public sign of unwillingness to make ever more sacrifices by women who by their innumerable voluntary war-time commitments - often done alongside a regular job - had turned themselves into relentless machines against Hitler. A meeting at the Albert Hall of 8,000 women from all over the country, the largest gathering of the whole war, might have alarmed a lesser man. Two hundred MPs signed a motion of protest and Bevin promised that no woman in this age-group would be forced to neglect her family.

Monica Capadose (née Bramwell)
"Despite her heavy load of regular voluntary commitments, making camouflage-netting, the RAF and 'Barra-boys' for baths, St Mary's Hall Canteen to run, British Legion to man, house-to-house collecting for National Savings, fire-watching on a rota, my mother (Joan Bramwell) also greatly enjoyed the company of a succession of delightful FANYs: (First Aid Nursing Yeomanry) drivers billeted on her at *Carters Cross*. But the straw that nearly broke the camel's back

was the requirement put upon her at one stage during the war, to undertake some form of paid employment. She chose to work for Miss Watts who ran a small cafe, 'The Old Way', just around the corner from Lodge Lane where to-day is Westerham Travel."

4 October 1943. WPC minutes:

Aid to China Fund: Mrs Papillon: the WVS do not organise flag days. Correspondence handed over to the Secretary of the WI.

3 November 1943. WI Archives. Maidstone.

Expenditures on the WI Balance Sheet for the year ending November 3 1943 include:-
Waste Paper Charities - £26.1.0.
War Risks Insurance -   £1.5.0.
Entertainment: Mrs Brunsden. Westminster Bank. Market Sq.
Drama: Mrs Mary Quirke. Red Cow House.
Handicraft: Miss Gosling. Farleyside. Farley Common. Assistant Handicraft: Mrs Violet Wells. Uplands. Pilgrims' Way.
Music: Mrs H. Steven. Squerryes Home Farm.
Produce: Mrs Constance Dascombe. Farley Lodge. Farley Lane.
Housekeeping Committee: Mrs Foskett. Ridgeway. Trotts Lane.

15 November 1943. WPC minutes:

Painting of kerbs with white lines: could this be speeded up? It was agreed that the Clerk would write to the County Surveyor on the subject, suggesting the use of 'cat's eyes' if possible.

3 January 1944. WPC minutes:

Consideration of the question of the re-erection of certain important sign posts throughout the district. Parish Council asked if they would care to prepare a list of the more important road junctions in the Parish where it is considered essential that sign posts should be re-erected as soon as possible. It was agreed that all the pre-war road signs are necessary, and it was suggested that they be re-erected at modern height - head-lamp level. Attention to be given to painting the kerbs and renewal of white line on the carriageway. 'Cat's-eye' studs are often removed by so much military traffic on the road, especially Bren Gun Carriers.

Cycling. Footpath. Darenth Towers, (Westerham Place):

O.C. Royal Air Force, Sundridge:
Orders will be issued to the effect that all personnel are forbidden to cycle along the footpath or to tamper with the gate.

12 January 1944. WI Archives. Maidstone.

Handicrafts: 319 garments knitted for the Merchant Navy.

Waste Paper Depot:
Six Tons was collected and sorted during the year.

Elizabeth Streatfeild
"At *Hosey Rigge* the only room in the house that was considered suitable for air raids was the downstairs bathroom where my father piled the Encyclopædia Britannicas all the way up the inside of the windows as defence against blast and flying glass."

John Warde
"Early in 1944 a huge 1000 lb land mine came down by parachute at the top of the (*Squerryes Court*) garden, exploding at surface level, doing a hell of a lot of damage and blowing out all the windows. On a sunny day you can still see splinters glittering in the gravel. One of my earliest memories is of my grandmother coming over to visit us and wandering round with a bucket picking up fragments of glass. That land mine in what we called 'the shake' also caused a number of the ceilings at *Squerryes* to fall down. The whole house must have gone up and down so that none of the doors would open or close properly afterwards. Some of our important Chinese plates stacked in a pile, must also have gone up and down as every one was broken in two and had to be repaired. After that we used to refer to things as having happened either before or after 'the shake.'"

Land mines were similar to sea mines and came down with a built-in parachute. Not only were they silent, but they landed so gently that the blast was not partially absorbed by impact with the ground as was the case with HE bombs, so did more damage.

John Warde
"At the beginning of the war we all used to go down to the cellars. I think I can just remember being carried down there. Later on they thought it would be just as safe if they shored up a room in a part of the house which has since been

demolished. In the housekeeper's room next to the kitchens, ash poles were set up to support the ceiling and a blast-wall was built about five yards in front of the window. It was half finished and we were all in that room when the land mine parachuted down. And we were in our beds in that room too when the 'doodle-bugs' arrived and a kind of glorified pheasant-shoot began with mobile anti-aircraft guns turning up to blaze away in the park and in the fields. The sound of gun-fire from the tall, skyward-pointing fingers of the Bofors kept us awake all night."

10 March 1944. Westerham Scout Records.

On Monday several of the senior Scouts acted as 'casualties' for the St John's Ambulance Brigade. The proceedings were most realistic and took place in the dim darkness of a deep cellar. It was a very instructive experience for all concerned and the Scouts are looking forward to a repetition of the 'incident'.
1944's Camp, 17th Sevenoaks. Westerham Junior HOBA.
Scout Troop had to be on Hosey Common as the whole of the South of England was a vast military camp busy with the invasion of Europe.

"All those Canadians had 'CANADA' written in capital letters across their arms, which even the little ones could manage to read. And in the playground at school we used to chant:-

Whistle while you work,
Ol' Hitler is a twerp,
He's half barmy
So's his army,
Whistle while you work.

And we used to tell the usual excruciating jokes...*'You know that static water tank just down the road? Well go and put your head in it three times and only take it out twice!'* And, *'Why does Hitler sleep with a net over his bed? Because he's afraid of our Mosquitoes!'*"

"A bomb fell on to a potato and turnip clamp in open fields and we kids had a great time as we were told they were free to anyone who could pick them up. The spoils of war, gathered in by lunch-time, as we were all excused morning school because of the raid."

"*Winterton Court* completed just before war broke out, had a sweet shop next-door to Smith's Gentlemens' Outfitters (to-day's Chow's Restaurant). In the run-up to D-Day, the two right-hand shop units, at that time un-let, were commandeered for the conversion of military vehicles for amphibious use. Exhaust pipes were installed vertically and the electrics and other vital engine parts were sealed and waterproofed with a black gooey mastic. They were parked out at the back near to-day's *Russell House* and Surgery car park."

Peter Finch
"At Charlie Sharp's Garage we re-charged batteries and in time I was put in charge of the Battery Shop. Then the Army started bringing their tank batteries to us. They were huge. An ordinary battery is heavy enough, but those were such massive things it took two men to handle them. I had to put them on charge in the morning and check their specific gravity. It was Charlie Sharp who signed my driving certificate form. We went up to Kent Hatch and he put me through my paces which was all that was needed in the way of a test in those days."

27 March 1944. WPC minutes:
Crockham Hill's Fire-Fighting Appliance:
Cr Colonel Robinson stated that the residents of Crockham Hill village are very much alarmed and anxious on account of the lack of fire-fighting appliances in that area. In view of recent occurrences they asked for the provision of a pump. It was agreed that the recommendation for a pump to be provided be submitted to the Area Officer of the National Fire Service. Strong complaints were made regarding the absence of any drainage system at Crockham Hill...this Council view with much apprehension and anxiety...the serious possibility and danger of an epidemic which might result. The prevailing conditions have been increased owing to the influx of the military and the evacuees.
Owing to the existing man-power position it is not possible to provide for the establishment of a trailer-pump station at every small centre of community - six enrolled members of the National Fire Service at Crockham Hill - and if a pump were provided it could be managed on one night a week only. Accommodation for pump necessary ...Major Marnham (of Chartwell Farm) said the reply was not satisfactory...It was agreed that he would interview the Head Warden.

In the event, he was to report that he had interviewed various people in the village with the following results:-

The Head Warden did not consider it was the Head Warden's business, the Head Fire Watcher did not appear capable and the Vicar was unable to do anything. The matter was left in abeyance.

"There was a lot of drinking going on. Westerham had so many pubs, the men were all waiting about, everything was ready for the 'off' and they had money in their pockets. They must have been pretty edgy too and 'browned off', so there were fights from time to time. Publicans had to cope with the occasional 'disturbance', the doctor might be called to attend and a Canadian was killed by another Canadian in a brawl outside the George & Dragon."

Peter Finch
"In 1942 I left the Scouts and joined the Army Cadet Corps. I was a big lad for 17, and even though I wore the Corps' uniform, I had to keep clear of some of the troops who would try to pick a fight with me. I wasn't yet able to join up, but that didn't stop them."

Monica Capadose (née Bramwell)
"My mother (Joan Bramwell) as a member of the WVS in 1944 was absent from Westerham for 2-3 weeks on a very secret mission. Having been asked if she would be willing to undertake some confidential war work, to which she had agreed - she was picked up by a chauffeur-driven car in which another woman (unknown to her) was already travelling and they were driven towards the south coast. During the journey they were given an envelope with instructions and having changed into another vehicle they arrived eventually at what she reckoned must have been somewhere in the Worthing direction.

It turned out to be a vast camp at which every kind of public service was represented. The military in the form of troops, the police, the Red Cross, the ARP, the WVS, the Civil Defence, the National Fire Service etc. What emerged was that the government (with D-Day looming), was making monumental preparations in the expectation that they might be required to receive possibly many thousands of hungry and traumatized French civilian refugees who might choose to return - in our empty troop carriers and tank landing craft no doubt - to take shelter in Britain as our troops advanced into their country.

In the event the *raison d'etre* for that enormous exercise in efficient provision, as we now know, was never to materialize. But with hindsight one can understand the total secrecy in which the whole enterprise had had to be undertaken."

* Malcolm is almost certainly referring to Pilot Officer Edward English who flew with 605 Squadron from Croydon during the Battle of Britain. On 7 October 1940 he was shot down over Westerham and killed when his Hurricane crashed and burned out at Park Farm, Brasted. English who was 28 is buried at Jesmond Cemetery, near his home town.

As D Day grew nearer, special constables played their part in checking civilians'
identity cards. Here they are at a barrier at Dairy Lane crossroads, Crockham Hill.
Freda McBride (then Wright) is proffering her papers. The tree is no longer there.

D-Day and Doodlebugs

Phil Johnson: "The build-up to D-Day was incredible. Lorries, tanks and tremendous activity. Practice gliders towing, and I remember seeing concrete barges on the Thames which were *'Mulberry'*."

Jean Hay

"On D-Day we were awoken by a thunderous roar from overhead and hurried downstairs and out into the garden. A never-to-be-forgotten sight greeted us in the form of hundreds of Lancaster bombers and American Flying Fortresses passing overhead in tight formation with Hurricanes and Spitfires escorting them. We realised at once where they were going and that the much- talked-of landing in France was actually taking place. We lay on our backs on the lawn at *Borde Hill* for nearly an hour watching and waving our handkerchiefs as they roared over us: and still they kept coming. A marvellous sight."

Don Adams

"They just went out in convoys. They vanished overnight. They absolutely vanished overnight and nobody knew they were leaving. My sister married one of those Canadians. He was stationed up somewhere on the Chart near the *Salt Box*. He used to come down home. They all used to come to meals and there was never any trouble. Sometimes after a few pints in the pub it got a bit noisy of an evening. But nobody had a car in those days. We all walked or used bikes so it wasn't dangerous like to-day. None of us could have afforded a car, even if there'd been any to be had, or any petrol."

Felicity Gladstone

"What was so amazing about D-Day was that everybody disappeared. They positively disappeared. And then we heard that they had all been ordered to go up north. Not in convoy but separately. They were then all to scatter and to make their way down separately, to *rendez-vous* in the south, clearly in the Portsmouth/ Southampton area. They weren't allowed to travel in convoy in case they should be spotted from the air heading for the ports of departure.

A little later, suddenly, along came some soldiers in a great big army truck, asking if they could stay the night with us. They were some of those troops who had been stationed in Crockham Hill before. So they spent the night at *Lewins,* and saying that they would be off in the morning and that like homing pigeons they had returned to us, they parked their huge army truck beneath the archway that runs under the house. It was not until after breakfast the next morning when we were waving them good-bye as they climbed aboard, that we realised that that truck was absolutely full of ammunition for France. A man had been mounting guard over it underneath our house all night. It really was a 'Dad's Army' war in so many ways."

Just a week after D-Day, on 13 June 1944, Hitler's secret 'Terror Weapons' began to arrive. The first pilotless aircraft, the flying bombs or 'doodlebugs' crossed the English Channel in the early hours of the morning. One crashed at Swanscombe, and 3,000 others followed, all directed at London. Also called 'buzz-bombs' the VI stood for *Vergeltungswaffe I,* 'vengeance weapon I' - with reference to the Normandy Landings. Intended to distract and frustrate us, forcing us to redirect our resources from the liberation of Europe, they had been in preparation in Germany since December 1943. But many of their launch-sites had been demolished by our bombing and were soon being over-run.

"With a range of 186 miles and propelled by a liquid fuelled rocket engine, V2's were 47 feet in length with a span of 10 feet. I couldn't believe the vastness of them till I saw one at the Imperial War Museum where I also found a V1 doodlebug, a German butterfly bomb and those incendiaries we used to collect for swapping at school."

"The close proximity of Biggin Hill to London brought it within the defensive barrage belt, and at the end of June 1944, the station was taken over by Balloon Command. The airfield lay right in the middle of 'Bomb Alley' and no fewer than six VI flying bombs crashed inside the airfield boundary."

"As the need for RAF men at Combe Bank receded, the Barrage Balloon men arrived. Overnight they filled the sky with what us kids saw as 'elephants'. Their arrival had all the excitement of the arrival of the Circus Big Top."

"In an attempt at protecting London, an enormous aerial arc of some 344 balloons now covered Westerham, Tatsfield and Biggin Hill and fields all around were dotted about with winches and tents and the sky with silver blobs, whose 'fins' rippled in the breeze. Sometimes they flew lower, sometimes higher. This became an on-going topic of conversation and we gave individual balloons names. Their raising and lowering by sweating crews heaving on the winches was a regular treat for us kids to watch. For our grown-ups they were a kind of air-raid barometer, except that none of us knew what they were raising or lowering them for. Their fat sides glowed like tiny silver specks that got all mixed up with the stars, and after a fine sunset, mysteriously, they remained pink long after the colour had disappeared from the sky."

Arthur Yeadon

15 June 1944 - the 'Alert' sounded about midnight ...an hour passed, no 'All Clear' and nothing had happened...my wife and I sat outside drinking mugs of cocoa...The searchlights had coned a plane, it was on fire but it came straight on, no evasive action, its tail was ablaze, there was a flash and in 20 seconds a terrific explosion. I thought nothing of it, just another Jerry hit by our guns and brought down...but when another came along, same route, same searchlight cone, same blaze on its tail, I began to think something was wrong...we sat there till it was almost daylight...But before I could get into bed hoping to get an hour or two's sleep, I saw another of the things and it seemed to be making straight for our house. It roared by, about a quarter of a mile away, a flash and crash simultaneously and I saw it go down near a house on the hillside to the West of me and the house was ablaze in a matter of seconds.

I flew downstairs and 'phoned Skinner and Bailey, got out the car and picked them up. We knew the incident was outside our area (in Surrey) but we went to give what help we could, knowing that it was a border line incident and a long distance from the nearest Godstone ARP Warden. I think this was the first buzz-bomb to fall in the area... It was a tragic incident...three people in the house, two were rescued almost unhurt, but the third, a lady, was burned to death in the fire and a fireman was electrocuted by his own axe coming into contact with a severed overhead cable, and it was feared that he would not pull round. Later I heard he had recovered, and I think he owes his life to Company Officer Colbourn of Westerham NFS who worked for half an hour with artificial respiration until the arrival of the ambulance.

Ethel 'Diamond' Charman (née Allen)

"Company Officer Colbourn was decorated for his life-saving initiative at an incident. With great presence of mind he used a pair of rubber boots as insulation and to protect his arms from the flames to rescue a Westerham firemen who was badly burned about the face and neck."

Mollie Couldrey (née Parker)

"Charles was away in the forces and I was living at *Farley Cottage* where we had a sequence of different batteries coming and going as neighbours at *Little Rosings* (now *Old Rosings)* which was used partly as an army canteen. When the first doodlebug came over in the early hours of the morning it was terrifying. All the men next-door promptly disappeared to see what the fearsome noise was all about, and what on earth had happened, leaving the cook behind on his own. My small daughter Jackie and I were sleeping on the ground-floor where there was a cupboard under the stairs, when suddenly there was a knock on my door. And there was this cook, wearing his tin hat with a fixed bayonet on his rifle, telling me that something terrible had just gone through the sky and that the others had all gone off and left him. Jackie was sound asleep, I had hurriedly put on my trousers, having sensed that something serious was happening and I invited him in for a cup of tea. And there he sat, still wearing that hat and still holding his rifle with bayonet at the ready, until I suggested he put it down and have a biscuit."

"One of those balloon things brought down a flying bomb behind farm buildings at Tatsfield. But Biggin Hill got it much worse than we did. One crashed on to a Nissen hut up there and killed three men. Curiously enough, Colonel Peter Nissen who designed the prototype for the huts ended his days at *Deepdale* on Westerham Hill, died in 1930 and is buried in Westerham Churchyard."

Beryl Bellingham (née Howard)
"An airman tipped the wing of a VI which then crashed in *Squerryes Park*, instead, as it would otherwise have done, on to the town."

"You can always tell where a balloon used to be. Nettles still grow where the crews had their rubbish heaps. Older local people connect individual flourishing patches of nettles with places where they remember balloon crews to have camped out with their balloons straining and tugging at their moorings. The balloon barrage to protect London thinned out a bit by the time it reached Crockham Hill, but I remember we had one close to the church and there was another at *Moat Farm*."

The Rev Oliver Fielding Clarke
Some people in a harvest field were machine-gunned one day by a low-flying enemy aircraft, but fortunately no one was hit. On another occasion (9 July 1943) a Nazi bomber dived through the clouds on the centre of the village, but, just as I was waiting helplessly for the worst, climbed back into the cloud and flew off to East Grinstead, thirteen miles away, where it released its bombs, killing a large number of people, mostly children in a cinema. Otherwise those middle war years were comparatively quiet. It was after D-Day that we had our worst experience.
The flying bombs were launched from platforms near the coast on the continent and never swerved from their course. When their engines cut out they fell and exploded and they were all timed to cut out over London. They seemed to come over about every twenty minutes and we were soon able to identify the various routes which crossed the parish.

Margaret Tulloch (née Johnson)

"A doodlebug crashed in the field next to *Fiddlers,* behind *Cathedral Cottage* on the Croydon Road. I just happened to see this strange thing streaking past the window of our house in Westbury Terrace. But without the usual flame in its tail I didn't immediately recognize it for what it was: a V1, arrived at the point to which its flame had driven it, which was now extinguished, and sloping towards the ground and a massive explosion."

Peter Steven

"There was a barrage balloon tethered just behind *Fiddlers* which caused a VI to slide down its cable and fall off it before it reached the ground. I was chasing butterflies across a field with Bernard Isted when we heard it coming and the engine stop. We dived for cover into a ditch, then heard the thing whistling. And you could hear them gliding through the air after the engine had stopped. Peeping out from the ditch we saw it heading North over the horizon of this field and then came the explosion. I was at Sevenoaks Prep. until September 1944, when I went on to The Judd, and on the day that the first doodlebug came over, when nobody knew what it was, we went straight home instead of catching the bus for school."

Don Adams

"If all was quiet, the 'barra-boys' might hand over some of their rations to local housewives who would add them to their own for a meal which they would all share together. This tended to happen if the 'boys' had 'lent a hand on the land' with hay-making or harvesting. The little extra pocket money didn't go amiss and some of the men were from farming families in any case, and were a Godsend at busy times, whilst their mates remained at their posts by their field telephone on the end of the balloon's hawser. We missed them when they went. They widened our horizons and made us feel more part of the war. I still have such happy memories of the barrage balloon crew in that field by Crockham Hill Church.

They lived in a tent there, looked after their truck and powered winch, and wound the balloon down when it needed topping up from the gas cylinders they carried. The balloons were supposed to make enemy planes fly higher and be less accurate with their bombing. When the V1's and V2's started coming over they added a second wire hawser with a sort of parachute on it. We used to go out there of an evening and sit and chat with them over a cup of cocoa. Looking back on it, I think our lives were really enriched by the war. Yes, I honestly believe that some of my happiest memories are of those war years."

"In fact the air at altitude, and not the gas in the main envelope could cause collapse and deflated fins as the barrage balloon ascended. Later in the war, re-deployment of launch-sites as our troops overran some of them caused the balloon barrage to be deepened around London so that Westerham bristled with them at the foot and along the top of the North Downs, on the approach to Biggin Hill."

Felicity Gladstone
"We had three cables in the neighbourhood of *Lewins* and each one brought down a flying bomb. One of those cables was left hanging in an oak tree until quite recently, because no-one could get it down."

Arthur Yeadon
Sunday 18 June 1944, we had a first class incident, the biggest we have had in the Sector. I was coming back from Sevenoaks on the bus...just past Brasted I heard the sound of a 'doodle' on its way...immediately overhead, very low...it was obviously going to have difficulty getting over Westerham Hill. For some reason it went into a vertical dive, there was a flash and a crash and the hillside west of Westerham Hill was enveloped in smoke and dust. I could not see where it had dropped but I knew it was not far from The Hill. *The bus seemed to crawl into Westerham and by the time I arrived on the scene, Dence and the rest of the gang were already on the job and had matters well in hand.*

The 'doodle' had hit a tree about 50 yards northwest of Durtnell's house (Betsoms) *which was in a pretty bad state and a cottage in the garden was a total wreck. The Durtnells and their two children were in bed and by a miracle none of them was hurt...Mr Durtnell caused some amusement by running around the garden with a bottle of brandy in one hand (for his own fortification) doing his best to catch his tame rabbits whose hutches had been blitzed...the most pitiful sight was their dog which had caught the full blast of a broken window and was lying there pitted with glass splinters. There was only one thing to do for the poor beast. There were about 40 Army lorries parked along the private road and most of these were damaged...they were supposed to be moving off the following morning but their departure was somewhat delayed. Two soldiers were hurt but these were dealt with by the Military authorities...Every house on Pilgrims Way from* Betsoms Farm *to the Waterworks was damaged in some way.*

Neville Wells
"The bomb that crashed on to *Betsoms* brought our *Uplands* lath and plaster ceilings down like a carpet in most rooms in the house, and my bedroom ceiling was open to the sky. We spent the rest of that night at Mr and Mrs Bill Cosgrove's and after that for about five weeks or so, at the Royal Oak in Sevenoaks

until we could return home. This was the stage of the war for me when I had been working for a few weeks at Charlie Sharp's between leaving *Charterhouse* and joining up. Father had had a shelter built in the garden at the start of the war which we had now stopped using. The cook, who worked during the day to feed the men on nearby balloon sites, was having his nights' rest disturbed in the tent as the men changed watch. They were on duty throughout the 24 hours. He had asked permission to use our shelter for sleeping in. It was that cook who was first on the scene after the doodlebug had landed and who hadn't expected to find anyone alive in *Betsoms* where mercifully all the Durtnell family survived.

"It was said that King George VI enjoyed visiting ack-ack units and watching them shoot down doodlebugs as they came over the Weald of Kent. But even more dramatic was the chance sight of one of our planes 'tipping' a VI rocket as it chugged on towards London, usually at around 380 mph. A small mid-wing monoplane with its single fin above the jet of orange flame, its fuselage filled with a ton of explosive, unless literally thrown off course or blown up in the air, it would travel straight towards its target with devastating results."

Certain types of aircraft such as the Tempest, the Meteor and the Typhoon, having speed and stout wings were particularly good for this dangerous manoeuvre of 'tip and run'. A plane's slipstream could upset the robot plane's gyro-control sending it plunging to earth - hopefully into open country. Or a daring pilot, if he could fly alongside and at the same speed as his target, might, by tilting one of his wings underneath that of the V1, send it hurtling downwards. A number of local people remember witnessing this courageous 'moving in for the kill' going on in the sky above them, and holding their breath...'on a wing and a prayer' as one said.

"I watched a Typhoon tip a V1 over, having flown right into a barrage balloon cable to do it. One Sunday morning this Typhoon took a chance with the cables and flew through them, caught up with the doodlebug, tipped it with his wing, banked away and the thing rolled over a couple of times and then exploded in the air. It must have exploded over what is now the M25 motorway no distance from where Churchill School is to-day. I was in The Paddock at the time and I saw our pilot having banked away, fly south again. Typhoons and Tempests were particularly able to do this: they had to be able to achieve the same speed as the flying bombs and to have strong wings because the pilots had physically to manoeuvre their aircraft so that the wings would cause them to turn over towards the ground. He couldn't possibly have seen those cables which were only about as thick as your finger. Flying at 400 or so miles per hour he must just have decided to chance it - though he surely would have seen the balloons floating above. Perhaps from the position of the balloons he thought he saw a gap and decided to take a gamble on getting through it without tangling with a cable."

Joan Thorneycroft (née Lelliott)
"I wonder what I would have done, 50 years ago, if I had been posted to Major Warde's Battery on the Norfolk coast. As it was, we (gunners in the ATS) were billeted in the Grand Hotel at Sheringham for three weeks whilst we went to Weybourne Practice Camp for firing practice. We had a three-week crash course to learn the new remote-control techniques for coping with the VIs. I remember seeing Helen Cassavetti as she then was, (now Hankey) striding across the parade ground at Park Hall Camp, Oswestry, where she was a sergeant in the ATS."

"There was one of those barrage balloons at the bottom of Pilgrims' Lane where it goes from Pilgrims' Way to *Pilgrim House*. We used to have an observation post in the turret of Westerham Church up in the bell tower. Two hours we did up there, and then we were relieved by another two Home Guards for their two hours."

Just occasionally what should have been another VI triumphantly notched up on the score-board of 'kills', went wrong. This happened when one was shot down over Crockham Hill.

Phil Johnson
"This incident is burned into my memory"...and in the memories of a number of local people who hurried to the scene to try to help.

"At 3.30 in the morning of Friday June 30th 1944 a V1 was on its deadly way to London. It was a lovely warm midsummer morning as my mother, my younger sister Barbara and I were standing on the porch of our cottage overlooking the Weald, watching the thing travelling towards us. My sister Marjorie had just returned from her fire-watching stint at *Little Court* where she had been on duty until 3.30. As she walked the short distance home she heard the dreaded chug-chug. They regularly passed over us en route for London, but this one appeared to be losing height, not so much toppling as proceeding in a fast fairly flat glide. We thought that as it was so low, it would just clear our house and then hit the hill behind us. Instead of this, it caught a thermal and lifted over the hill with flak coming up all around it from an anti-aircraft battery over at Four Elms where the guns had opened up. Then, travelling on the still air we heard a cheer rise up from the crew as the wretched thing cut out.

It seemed ages (it was by then 3.37) before we heard the explosion, and my sister guessed where it had crashed. She was friendly with Pam, the young daughter of Mr Smith, the gardener at *Weald House*. So she and I set off immediately to investigate. It was devastating. The only other person immediately to reach the scene of the disaster was our neighbour farmer Moore of *Froghole Farmhouse*.

I gave him a hand, holding up one end of a joist that had come down right along a line of cots, using a timber lever whilst he pulled the children out. It seemed a long time before the fire and rescue service arrived and they promptly kicked me out. My sister's young friend who was pregnant was unhurt in the gardener's cottage, but she herself will never forget seeing one of the staff there, with a leg blown off. To this day she is haunted by that tragic sight and has always wondered how that poor girl had managed to escape from the building, visualising that she must have been hurled clear by the explosion. As for me, I got back home later in the morning, which I also remember well, as I got penalised for being late for school that day."

Marjorie Thomson (née Johnson)
"Phil and I hurried up to *Weald House* through the woods, expecting to find that it was the trees that were on fire. There was no sound at all other than the crackling and roaring of the fire and the screams of that poor young girl lying in the drive with her leg blown off. Even though I had attended first aid classes in the village, I was really not able to do anything for her except stay with her. She must have been a nurse or a member of the domestic staff aged about 20 or so. I never heard if she survived or what became of her. But Phil was right in it, though when the rescue team arrived they said he was too young and sent him away."

Don Adams
"Doodlebugs were going over all night long. You got used to them like everything else. We were on Home Guard duty over Bough Beech way when suddenly someone said 'that one's over Crockham Hill way', and we saw a bright glow in the sky. In the blackout it was going mad that fire. Lieutenant Gladstone rang his wife at *Lewins* from a phone box, so we knew before we set off just where it was. Volunteers were asked for in case we could help with all those little mites, and everyone climbed on board the truck. We were trying to help by shifting bricks out of the way when a specialist rescue squad arrived from Sevenoaks. By that time so many people had rushed to see what they could do that they asked us all to back off so they could listen for voices under the rubble. We could see where some of the babies had been laid out on the grass,

Weald House, Crockham Hill which was used by London County Council as a nursery school. Here, 22 of the 30 children, all aged under five, were killed or died later in hospital. Eight of the 11 nurses or domestic staff were also killed and the others were seriously injured. Many of those in the building were trapped by debris and only a few adults had been found by the afternoon. It was several days later before all the bodies were recovered.

This photograph was taken while rescue work was still in operation at Weald House. The chimney stack is all that remains of the nursery and the damaged building in the background is the gardener's cottage.

One of the domestic staff who was killed by the flying bomb was 30-year-old Catherine Inwood, whose two-year-old son Peter was living in a nursery at Little Mariners and mercifully missed the explosion. Peter (now Findley) was adopted by a family in Gateshead and grew up knowing nothing about the incident at Weald House until, at the age of 50, he decided to try and find out how his mother died. His investigations brought him to Westerham where he met Geoff and Betty Hoath who directed him to the re-built house at Crockham Hill. He also met Emma Norris who worked at Little Mariners in 1944 and visited Edenbridge churchyard where a memorial stone marks the names of those who died. It was Kent's most tragic incident of the war but we couldn't do anything, so we all just went back to our day's work."

Some 30 children, all of them under five, from a London County Council nursery school, which had earlier been destroyed by incendiary bombs, were evacuated from the London Docks area to the 'safety' of the country. When demolished by a V1 rocket, rescuers described the carnage and the garden full of twisted metal, cots in which babies had been sleeping, tiny shoes and vests, soft toys, and diminutive pink and blue blankets which were scattered over a wide area, hanging from trees in the garden and far out into the woods and fields.

In the new Cemetery behind Edenbridge Parish Church a memorial commemorates the 8 adults, of the 11 nurses and domestic staff, and 21 babies killed in the disaster.

IN MEMORY OF THE NURSES, STAFF AND CHILDREN OF THE LCC RESIDENTIAL SCHOOL AT WEALD HOUSE CROCKHAM HILL. KILLED BY ENEMY ACTION ON JUNE 30 1944.

The name of this house has been changed twice since then. A service was held at Holy Trinity, Crockham Hill in July 1994... 'To commemorate the 50th anniversary of the destruction of *Weald House* and the consequent loss of life.' Amongst the congregation was a woman who had survived the tragedy but who still limps as a result of her injuries, and Peter Inwood, son of 30-year-old Catherine Inwood, a member of the domestic staff who was killed in the disaster. He survived because he had had an infectious childhood illness at the time and had therefore been segregated and left at another house in Crockham Hill commandeered by the LCC. Peter was adopted by a family in Gateshead and grew up knowing little about the incident at *Weald House* until, at the age of 50, he decided with his wife to try to find out how his mother had died. Gradually the pieces of the jig-saw came together when his investigations led him to Crockham Hill after a chance link, through Kev Reynolds, with someone who had known and worked with his mother at the time of the disaster.

Freda McBride (née Wright)
"I was fire-watching at *Pilgrim House* when that monstrous thing crashed down on *Weald House*, but I couldn't go home. I had to wait till six o'clock. You stayed there for twenty-four hours if you were fire-watching. They had wooden bunks for us in wooden chicken-house-type buildings. The staff lived in some too, with one set aside for late night fire-watchers. There would be about a dozen of us at a time. On the occasion of an attack on Biggin Hill, cycling home from *Pilgrim House* I had just got as far as Westerham station when a Warden came out and said 'the siren's gone, you must come inside.' I was supposed to be

going on to the dentist, but he was adamant, and like everybody else he saw out in the road, I had to go down into their shelter (at the entrance to what to-day is The Flyer's Way) till the all-clear went."

Gladys Ivey (née Whitmore)
"A whole train-load of us set off on *The Flyer* for Dunton Green, London and then Dawlish. But I wasn't happy to be away from my husband (Ted Ivey) who was signalman at Westerham station. If he had not been in a reserved occupation and had been away from home, I might have stuck it out, with all those doodlebugs coming over. They had dear little cottages down there for us, but they were overrun with rats and I really couldn't stand it. In the end we only stayed for two or three weeks. We were all of us mothers with small children."

Ivory Moffatt
"After the disastrous bombing of *Weald House*, our little school was evacuated, including a few children who had stayed on with us from Peckham. Miss Cutbush and Miss Merkl remained in Westerham and I was put in charge of the evacuation of Westerham's children. We travelled down to Dawlish from Oxted where I was delighted to find that the Hosey boys were going with us.

Some of our parents had come to help and we took several churns of milk with us for the journey. We picked up children from St Mary's at Oxted, and the Haberdashers' children who had already been evacuated out of London, and all their staff, and the Edenbridge children with two of their teachers. All along the line we collected little groups of children from tiny stations like Chiddingstone and Hever, and I hadn't even been told for certain where we were going until I got my marching orders at the last minute by phone. Everything had been shrouded in secrecy yet, somehow, all along the line we were fed by the WVS at the various stations where we were offered buns and pieces of cake and lemonade.

When we left the train at Dawlish we were much envied by the other schools whose children were going on to Newton Abbott which was not 'the seaside'. They unlocked the doors and let out the Westerham and Crockham Hill children. Some of whom had never seen the sea before and couldn't get over the fact that it was moving as it hurled itself up and over the railway track.

But we were back in Westerham about six months later, a number of parents having travelled down to Dawlish to visit their children for the weekend, and because they found that they hadn't 'settled', took them back with them. Anyhow we were all home again just in time for the V2 rocket on Madan Road.

On Saturday nights the Canadian troops used to get up to all sorts of pranks such as when they climbed up - goodness knows how they did it - and put a chamber-pot on General Wolfe's head and on another occasion draped a string of sausages over the tip of his sword. Perhaps after all, Westerham was a more exciting place in which to be spending those war-time days."

Phil Johnson

"I was never on the petrol pumps. I was always round the back in the workshop. But I do know there was a lot of fiddling went on in the front - all very hush-hush and covered up and not for my ears. Everyone had an Austin 7 and there was a tremendous shortage of new main bearings (MRJ 1¼ inch). If we got one, we would fit it to the car that least needed it. We could then move that into the next car down and so on - three or four for the price of one. Tyres, especially 450 x 17 (Ford Morris) and 300/360 x 19 (motor bikes and Austin 7). Anything went, even stuffing them with hay as a last resort. You couldn't see some of the inner tubes for patches. A lot of people would keep more than one car registered - some had several. They would then not use the big cars but keep the petrol ration for the small runabout."

Peter Fuller

"We were at my grandparents' house, *Kenwood* where we live now, when in the middle of the night some 16 or so bombs crashed down on to the Buckham Thorns and The Slip area. Not one of them exploded which was a miracle as many of them landed within just feet of each other. Ralph and Winifred Childs were in bed at *Ralwin* where Phil and Jean Johnson now live when a bomb came in through the north wall and burst out on the south side, but not before it had caused Ralph to suffer a broken leg. Along with several other Special Constables, my father Hugh Fuller went up there and covered the bomb, which had landed on the grass in front of the house, with sand-bags. The whole area was cleared, and our family went to Uncle Cyril Fuller who was living at the shop in the High Street at the time. There was one bomb just outside the back door here, another only a few feet from the frontdoor of *Chevington*, my parents' house next door, another in what to-day is Mrs Pyke's garden at *Little Orchard* and at *Northcote//Southcote* in The Slip, they had one straight down the chimney."

Ion Calvocoressi

"*Court Lodge* was commandeered as a Canadian officers' mess throughout the war years and the large barn which had housed a badminton court was used as their tank and vehicle repair and maintenance workshop. The wooden floor was dug up and concreted over and the tanks were driven straight out of the barn and through the lovely old duck pond close to the house. The late Ted Drapper remembered the damage that this caused to the foundations of what had been a well-filled pond which no longer holds water as well as it used to. In the 'seventies when they were excavating about 200 yards north of the house to

An unexploded bomb was also discovered in the 'seventies when a swimming pool was being built in a field at *Courtlands*, precisely where Dr Aidan Long had for years had his garden bonfire. These two must have been part of the same stick which mercifully never exploded.

"A large HE bomb fell on the old football ground near *Court Lodge*. In all, some 15-18 unexploded bombs fell on Westerham, notably in the Paddock. We kids soon got our priorities right when what our Mum took to the air raid shelter was Dad's teeth, the insurance policies and a bottle of brandy for emergencies."

Gladys Richards (née Moore)
"I worked as a member of the wartime staff of Mr Ronald Vestey. Living at *Grosvenor House* I just crossed the bottom of Hosey Hill with my bike, in through those big iron in Quebec Square, I just crossed the bottom of Hosey Hill with my bike, in through those big iron gates and rode up the drive. His permanent Union Cold Storage staff were evacuated from Smithfield to spend the weekdays living and working at *The Valance*. They went home on The Flyer at the weekends. We all had to do something, so I counted the coupons (points) sent in from butchers all over the country. We used to get enormous bundles of them, the largest being from a firm called Allied Suppliers. There were no supermarkets then of course, so they distributed to all the little butchers' shops.
The military set up great rolls of barbed wire at the bottom of the garden, backing on to the wood. There were dragons' teeth anti-tank pointed spikes stored in what today is The Old House at Home's car park where two cottages, adjacent and attached to the pub, had been taken down just before the war, as well as a gun pointing up Vicarage Hill. And the floor of the clubroom above the pub was reinforced with stout props, ready to support a gun emplacement. When the V2 crashed on to Madan Road, all our windows were blown out and my husband retrieved a large piece of the casing of the rocket from our garden."

"At Verralls Corner, at the top and bottom of Vicarage Hill and at the top of the London Road, the army had dug holes in the road, and then capped them. Had invasion occurred, the holes were all ready to take the stout concrete posts or dragons' teeth that were stored close by".

Moorhouse works, Westerham showing the NAAFI supplies depot which became Redlands PLC.

Madan Road rocket — with victory in sight

John Warde: "Park Cottages were farm and estate cottages, one of which was occupied by Sunny Geal who worked up at the sand-pit. He had been a Sergeant in WW1, was one of my great heroes and a good ferreter who used to take me ferreting with him. He was also a part-time keeper and used to man a little petrol pump in a pump-house we had up at the sand-pit for pumping water out of it after heavy rain. He often used to spend the night up there and this was how he began to take note of the habits of German planes that seemed to him to be avoiding going on to bomb London."

For most people the tip and run raids of 1942-43 were the last rolls of a receding storm. But in South-East England the storm returned in 1944 in a peculiarly terrorising form. A flying bomb that was shot down or brought down was just as lethal as one which crashed when its fuel ran out. And soon there would be the V2s as well.

16 June 1944. Hosey School Records.
Three pilotless planes passed over and exploded.

The Rev Oliver Fielding Clarke
One of the attempts made to intercept the 'doodlebugs' in our part of the country was to put up a huge screen of barrage balloons, the hope being that the cables would catch them. The sky seemed to be full of large aluminium-coloured sausages. During this phase of operations one of the more opulent of our parishioners was being taken to the station by our local butcher, who was also the village taxi-driver. 'Do you think, Mr B', she said anxiously, 'that if one of those things hit a balloon cable it would come down on us?' 'It would,' replied our butcher, 'and we should be very pleased to think that a few deaths here might save a street full of people in London'. However our balloon caught nothing, though I captured two RAF NCOs involved in the operation, for the sacrament of confirmation.

The Rev Charles Steer
During the summer of 1944 the 'flying bombs' launched from the Pas de

Calais were a source of a great deal of damage in the neighbourhood, being in the direct line for London...The immense concentration of barrage balloons did not add to the local sense of security, though it prevented many of the bombs penetrating to do damage in more thickly populated areas. The only fatality in the Parish (Limpsfield) *was a young mother who, with her husband was sleeping on the top of her Morrison Shelter - a sort of large steel dining-table with wire netting sides, which was erected in a very large number of houses and is known to have saved a great many lives. Two of the bombs landed, at a considerable interval, on almost the identical spot at the Horns in Staffhurst Wood, destroying one house and badly damaging two others; by the Grace of God these failed to do any harm to the huge ammunition dump which occupied the whole of the wood; they might have caused an immense disaster. It was therefore with real thankfulness that we heard of the success of the D-Day landings and of the gradual conquest of the Pas de Calais.*

In early July 1944 school children were once again evacuated. In their own air-space, the British struggled with how to defend civilians from this new deadly weapon. From mid-July a three-tier system of defence was in operation. Along the coast were amassed thousands of guns, many were directed by radar and fired shells with proximity fuses. Despite flying on a fixed course, the VI, thanks to its small size and high speed proved an elusive target. But the rate of kills rapidly improved. Between the coast and the outskirts of London the fighters had a free hand. In what became known as 'Doodle-bug Alley' the fighters tried to shoot down the missiles over the more thinly populated countryside.

The country's third and last line of defence, thousands of barrage balloons assembled along the North Downs. Their cables formed a steel net in the sky ready to ensnare bombs that had got through the artillery and the fighters. The flaming exhausts of the flying-bombs made a striking sight after dark. They also provided a target for the defending gunners and fighters. But still the VI's kept coming.

29 June 1944. Girls' School Records.

Owing to the frequency of air attacks the two Junior Girls' classes now work entirely in the shelters, having moved tables and chairs in there.

6 July 1944. Girls' School Records.

Children are to have facilities for evacuation to a safer district, (Dawlish in Devon).

Mary Kenward (née Petty)

"Aged nine I joined a group of Westerham youngsters to travel down to Dawlish as evacuees at a stage of the war which, because of the V1s and V2s, was beginning to be dangerous once again. I went with my brother, and we stayed there for nine months and came back about a month before the V2 Rocket crashed on to Madan Road. We lived at number 126 and my mother had just picked her baby up from his cot when shattered glass covered everything.

Still, we were glad to be back. We hadn't wanted to go in the first place and they had split us up. My brother wasn't with the same family as I was and I missed Westerham where we had been having an exciting war. There was always something going on here and I used to enjoy going out with my brothers looking for pieces of shrapnel. These had a razor-sharp edge that cut like a knife and were quite dangerous to handle. Somehow we all just seemed to know where to go looking for shrapnel. Someone said they'd found an arm up on the hill, but it could just have been, showing-off.

We were all young then and I reckon our parents protected us from much of what was going on. What we got, and I shall never forget, was the excitement of those war years. In the long school holidays a whole crowd of us used to jump on the trailer towed by Bob Steven's tractor and pick stones up off the fields around *Force Green Farm*. We got paid pocket-money at the end of the week for making little heaps of the stones. Then we used to go straight up to Sherry's shop at the top of Madan Road with our coupons and spend it on sweets, or to Master's on the corner of South Bank where we also sometimes sheltered in their cellar. And we used to go round to *Oak Lodge*. There was a Yorkshire regiment there at one stage and when they moved out the Canadians moved in, and they used to give us chocolate and what they called 'candies'."

Rosamond Pyke (née Curtis)

"I had been in the MTC, driving for the Ministry of Supply, the only member of my family still in England. My husband Tom was in the Eighth Army in North Africa and our two children were evacuated to Canada. In the spring of 1944, with the end of the war in sight I bought *Squerryes End* in Crockham Hill for them all to return to. The V1s started at this time but the house survived. It had been requisitioned by the Army, had been a Sergeants' Mess but was now empty. There were broken windows, the roof was damaged, the oak doors had been used as darts boards, but the Army had kindly left a little coal. By an extraordinary coincidence Greville Spencely, whom I had driven at the Ministry of Supply, turned out to live a few hundred yards away (at *Spencelys*) and he very kindly organised my War Damage claim and got Durtnells to do my repairs. But every time a V1 or V2 fell in the neighbourhood the workmen disappeared for days if not weeks. My heart sank when I heard that last explosion in Madan Road. It seemed unreal to be meeting two completely strange little girls aged nine and six, and rather devastating to be greeted with 'I wanna drinka warra.' VE Day was to me most memorable for looking down into the valley and seeing the lights in Edenbridge, and to the north a glow from the lights of London."

"In 1944 a VI landed in a field behind Westerham's British Legion clubhouse in Mill Lane, where on 9 June 1928 Diana Churchill had laid the foundation stone. It did some damage to the building, but there is little sign of this 'incident' to-day."

25 July 1944. Hosey School Records.

The school is now surrounded with a balloon barrage which extends for miles in all directions.

Phil Johnson
"When I was living at Crockham Hill, I used to help look after Fred Baxter, the local butcher cum taxi-driver's two Armstrong Siddeley 14 HP's and Morris Major. The Siddeleys were always in trouble with big ends and it was my job to lie underneath and close the bearings up. The sump was held up by 42 x ¼in bolts, nuts and washers. I knew every one. Fred also had a charging board out the back for radio accumulators, 2d a charge.
When in 1944/5 we moved to Westerham we lived in Captain Douglas Evison's flat above his Wolfe Garage on the Green: flush toilets, electricity, gas, taps and all.We had four 500 gallon tanks behind the garage and four pumps, and there was a thriving Black Market."

28 August 1944. WPC minutes:

Lighting: In view of the possibility of lighting the street lamps, it was agreed that a meeting of the Committee be held, and that Mr Manley of the Electricity Company be asked to attend to discuss types of lighting and a possible future contract.

Gordon Edgar
"When a doodlebug was brought down by a barrage balloon cable over the farm, the thing exploded, scattering hundreds of small pieces of twisted wire which it proved impossible completely to gather up. This was on a *Court Lodge Farm* field along Pilgrims' Way. In due course these found their way into the straw and animal feed causing disastrous damage to livestock, nearly all of those affected having to be slaughtered. We used to let all those little incendiaries that fell on to the fields just burn themselves out. But one night a lot landed all in amongst the trees in a wood on 60-acre field, to the right of Hog-Trough Hill,

The scene at Court Lodge farm, Pilgrims Way where a doodlebug (V1 flying bomb) was brought down by a barrage balloon, scattering pieces of twisted metal and wire all over the fields. In 1944/5 RAF Biggin Hill was the headquarters of Balloon Command and the skies above Westerham were full of balloons which looked smooth and silver, especially against the blue sky. There were balloon tragedies at Brasted and at Biggin Hill where a V1 was brought down by a cable and exploded on top of a Nissen hut standing on the airfield. Three airmen were killed.

and they created a sort of dramatic firework display."

Then on the evening of the 8 September 1944 the era of the V2 rocket began. Being supersonic they were impossible to detect. Travelling at three times the speed of sound, there was no warning.

16 October 1944 WPC proposed that the Clerk be instructed to send a telegram of congratulation to the Prime Minister on his 70th birthday.

Edward (Ted) Turner
"I worked at a garage called 'Brittain's Engineering' in Peckham in London, making Bailey bridges for sending to France for the Invasion. These were portable bridges consisting of a series of great prefabricated sections. They had hydraulic floats so that when they were thrown across the water they would stay afloat. The troops would build two of them at a time. One that could be seen by the enemy as it was being assembled, and which they would even then be planning how best to demolish, as they had the original permanent bridge...and a second Bailey bridge which would be constructed about one foot below the water by our divers. While the Germans were watching the building of the first bridge...further down the river Allied troops would be assembling that second, under-water bridge which would be used by our tanks and military vehicles. They must have appeared to be driving, biblically, on water.

We were also making 'jettison', auxiliary fuel tanks for fighter planes to carry extra fuel to enable them to fly further into Europe and still be able to get back home. Once refuelling facilities were established over there, the Westerham Brewery used to fill those auxiliary non-returnable petrol tanks with Westerham Ales for our troops in Europe. Black Eagle lorries delivered it in barrels to Biggin Hill where the auxiliary dual-purpose tanks were filled with Bitter on one side and Mild on the other. We made them of 16 gauge metal with baffles for safe landing, the RAF's version of the brewer's dray.

Group Captain 'Johnnie' Johnson DSO, DFC.
Back in England, some ingenious mind had modified the bomb racks slung under each wing...Daily, this modern version of the brewers' dray flew across the Channel and alighted at St Croix. The beer suffered no ill effects from its unorthodox journey and was more than welcome in our mess.

Ted Turner
"Brittain' Engineering moved to Westerham a couple of weeks after VE day, setting up as a garage across the road from Charlie Sharpe's in the High Street. I moved to Westerham with the firm and we went on making those auxiliary petrol tanks for jettisoning, but double-sized for use on larger aircraft in the Jap war which was still continuing."

20 November 1944. WPC. A fund was proposed to welcome home men and women of the parish serving in HM Forces.

Cr Streatfeild complained of the condition of the road across Farley Common. It was being cut up very badly by the tanks.

30 January 1945. WI archives. Maidstone.

Handicrafts: 345 garments have been knitted by members for the Merchant Navy. They have also been knitting for the liberated countries.

By the end of the war an entry reads:

'Letters have been sent to MP requesting more Women Police in Kent Constabularies.' The WI had also been contributing towards a nationwide 'Water and Sewerage Survey.' The object of the survey was to carry out the resolution on water and other public services passed at the National Federation of

Westerham ale for the troops in Europe. Black Eagle lorries delivered it in barrels to Biggin Hill, where auxiliary dual-purpose tanks on fighter planes were filled with mild on one side, bitter on the other.

Women's Institutes Annual General Meeting in 1943. The information collected on a national scale was in the end to provide valuable evidence. All had had to be collected and collated by March 1944.

Sunday 11 March 1945, a lovely sunny morning is still remembered by many Westerham people in as many different ways. For just after 10 o'clock, a V2 rocket crashed down on to Madan Road - one of the last to fall anywhere in Britain.

Malcolm Taylor

"As a 12-year-old paper-boy I was delivering newspapers up Vicarage Hill for Mr Bennett when I heard the rocket crash. I was half-way up the hill and soon realised that it had come from the direction of my home in Madan Road, so threw my bag of papers to an old chap who lived in Mill Street as everyone started coming out of their houses. Shrapnel and dust were whirling around as we dashed down the Brasted Road and I cycled madly along the footpath beside *Darenth Towers* and into the Market Field. At the top of Madan Road by the Corn Store (now George Elliott Ltd) I slipped through where they were setting up a road block and police cordon. Amazingly at home all was well and the massive explosion I had heard in Vicarage Hill, for them, had just been a kind of 'WHOOSH' with coats and things being blasted off hooks behind doors. When eventually I got back to Vicarage Hill, I found that the old chap had finished delivering my papers for me."

Gladys Ivey (née Whitmore)

"My father was blown across the road by the force of it. Our area had been enjoying a quiet spell so, to give them a break, we had invited my cousins down from Ilford where they had been having a terrible time with the bombing. But sadly as my cousin was standing by the window watching her little boy playing outside, the rocket crashed and the child was hurled backwards shattering the glass of the window and causing the poor woman to lose an eye.

Further along the road at number 80, George Blake, head wash house man at the Westerham Laundry was killed instantly in his garden. He had earlier complained of an unexploded bomb that he reckoned had gone to earth somewhere out there. But the bomb-disposal experts had not been able to locate it, though George had continued to insist that it was surely there ...and there are one or two, notably Malcolm Taylor and Geoff Hoath who to this day say that George Blake just before he died, whispered how distressed he was that his garden fork had set off the unexploded bomb he had always known was in his garden.

George Blake was the only victim of the Madan Road rocket but seven were seriou

jured and scores had lucky escapes. The blast caused damage to more than 300 homes.

*The Madan Road rocket blast on 11 March, 1945 could be heard for miles around.
The rescue operation was quickly into top gear and after the debris had been cleared
up, tarpaulins were provided to cover the roofs of the homes damaged in the blast.
The WVS set up their inquiry point and provided comfort and cups of tea for helpers
and residents. Those who have been identified in this photograph are Mr Wells and
Percy Geal, the Brasted cobbler in the background. In the foreground Peter Wells,
Tommy Martin, Ethne Lockyer, Helen Godfrey, Patricia and Pamela Boakes (twins),
Audrey Martin, June Chilman and one of her children and Anthony (Nobby) Moseley.*

Mollie Cosgrove who at that time had only been working for Dr Hay at his home-based surgery at *Borde Hill* since the 8th January, heard the explosion at her home on the Green.

"I had gone to bed with a horrible cold, a hot-water-bottle and a couple of aspirins when I heard the explosion. I shot out of bed, and together with one of the RAF boys we had billeted with us, decided that the great pall of smoke ːemed to be over the Bloomfield Terrace area where Dad had gone to his allot-ºt to get some onion-sets. Mother was off immediately and I rushed to Dr ʀay's house. Mrs Hay was relieved see me because her husband in his dash to see what he could do, had gone without his glasses, so could I take them.

I found him at the top of Madan Road and told him that I had opened up the Women's Institute as a first aid post and had told several Red Cross people I'd met on the way to go there immediately. Then Mr Hepworth, the Manager of Boots the Chemist (to-day's chemist occupies the same building) turned up with a car-load of cotton wool, lint etc., everything we could want in that way, and unloaded it all on to the stage. I asked him how he would know how much we should owe him. His answer was to use whatever we needed and he'd see what was left over and work it out after that, which would be perfectly alright.

Nurse Ford came down and we soon had the casualties for stitching assembled in the Guide Hut. They were all dealt with and away by about one o'clock. Three went to hospital and I think we dealt with sixty-one at the WI Hall. Little Edythe Curtis was badly injured but had been taken to hospital and of course Mr Blake was killed instantly. After that, Dr Hay ran a surgery every morning at the WI Hall until Dr Roffey from Bessels Green rang through to say that Dr Hay had had no right to attend the incident, as he himself had been appointed to deal with all war-time casualties in the area. Four houses were damaged beyond repair and at least 50 others needed work done on them."

Betty Pointon (née Boniface, later Mrs Victor Hobbis)
"I was living with my parents-in-law at 30 Madan Road when the rocket landed. I had just taken my little son Michael who had been sleeping in his cot, through to his grandparents' bedroom that Mothering Sunday morning, whilst I went through to make us all a cup of tea. I was dusting round by the window when suddenly it flew past me with great pieces of shattered glass landing on the cot upstairs. It was a miracle that he wasn't in it."

June Smith (née Jenner)
"I belonged to the Junior Red Cross with Mrs Duggan as our Commandant, so we had to go down there immediately and fill hot-water-bottles. There was chaos and chickens flapping about all over the place. Most of us were children from St Mary's C. of E. School."

"Everyone was very touched that Mrs Churchill came down from London by car that very afternoon to see for herself what had happened, and to sympathise with the people of Westerham. She brought with her a big box of chocolates, a present to her from Stalin, and handed them all around amongst the children."

Grace Hamblin
"I think that this box must have been one of the many presents showered on Mrs Churchill at the time that I accompanied her to Russia when she was Chairman of the Red Cross Aid to Russia Appeal. And they probably came from Madame Molotov's own chocolate factory in Moscow.

We were therefore in Moscow on VE Day and left for home just a few days later on May 11th. But there was so much work to be done on our return that I didn't accompany Mrs Churchill on that visit she paid to Madan Road. Nor for the same reason did I come down on the week-end visit to Chartwell when Mr Churchill stopped off on the Green to address the people of Westerham."

Joan Myhill (née Kimber)
"A pony and trap delivering milk along New Street was just going past when the rocket fell on Madan Road. The explosion was so terrific that the unfortunate animal bolted around the corner, along Westbury Terrace and up towards the allotments on Farley Common. Fortunately it was caught and held by Grandad and my young son Peter."

19 March 1945. WPC minutes:

A telegram received from London dated 11 March 1945:

TO THE CHAIRMAN OF THE PARISH COUNCIL WESTERHAM KENT PLEASE EXPRESS MY SYMPATHY TO THE SUFFERERS FROM THIS MORNING'S INCIDENT AND MY THANKS TO THE RURAL CONTROL AND ALL OTHER HELPERS FOR THEIR EXCELLENT WORK
WINSTON CHURCHILL

In reply:

TO THE PRIME MINISTER 10 DOWNING STREET LONDON ON BEHALF OF THE PARISH I THANK YOU FOR YOUR KIND MESSAGE OF SYMPATHY STOP THIS IS VERY ENCOURAGING TO ALL SUFFERERS WHO ACCEPTED THE POSITION WITH CHARAC-TERISTIC FORTITUDE AND TO ALL WHO HELPED SO SPLENDIDLY THROUGHOUT THE DAY

Ted Ivey

"*The Flyer* was not damaged by that rocket, but track was buckled alongside Madan Road and I had to alert the station-master at Dunton Green who had in fact heard the explosion and had reacted accordingly."

Towards the end of the war, to ease the desperate shortage of housing and allow young couples to have homes of their own, 12 prefabricated houses were put up at the end of Madan Road. Designed to last for ten years and intended as a cheap and temporary solution to the post-war demand for housing, 'prefabs' have confounded their creators by their durability and popularity. Proving to be remarkably resilient and surviving in many transformations they are to-day an endangered species of nostalgic interest. But Westerham's 'prefabs' were in due course demolished to make way for new houses to be built along to-day's Ash Road.

19 March 1945. WPC discussed the threadbare and waterlogged roads,and *Miss Cutbush, Headmistress of St Mary's Infants School complained of a report in the press that 'children have to sit about in school with wet footwear. The Clerk was requested to reply to the effect that the Council are concerned only with the state of the roadway.*

SRDC: .....anticipated the roads would be made up under the Private Street Works Act at the cessation of hostilities.

A hearty vote of thanks to Mrs Darkin and her helpers at the Library.

"As a greater number of convoys were now getting through, local fruit shops became more exotic until the great day came when the first five-foot-long banana box reached Westerham station. But prised open by Mr Hollingworth with his claw-hammer, inside, instead of the five-foot-long banana that I as a small child who had never before seen a banana had been anticipating, there were just disappointing rows of little yellow hands with green finger-tips."

"Before that, we used to boil up turnips, let them get cold and mix in some of our precious sugar ration. The grown-ups told us it gave the same taste as bananas."

Joy Edgar (née Herbert)

"My father was Manager of the Westerham and Edenbridge privately-owned Gas Light & Coke Co. We lived in the shadow of the gasometer at the out a deep reinforced shelter because of the [illegible] kind igniting the vast quantity of gas stored alongside us.

People used to collect their coke from our gasworks in sacks, wheelbarrows and carts till well after the war, and children with whooping-cough (myself included) used to be put to stand close to the (gas) 'purifier'. This was supposed to have medicinal properties that relieved the symptoms of what in those days could be a serious illness against which there was no protective innoculation. It had a really horrid 'rotten' smell that 'purifier'.

The 403 bus from Westerham to Croydon used to pass our door and stop at the bottom of Farley Lane. Unbeknown to the bus company, if there was a raid on in Croydon when the last bus was due to leave Westerham, the driver and conductor would bed down and spend the night with us. It just didn't seem sensible to take an empty bus into the middle of an air raid."

Arthur Yeadon
Skinner had rather an unfortunate experience with an escaped balloon, the cable got itself tied up with one of his apple trees and it dragged that apple tree out by the roots and made a much better job of it than he could ever have hoped to have done. Unfortunately, it was one of his best trees, and he had no particular wish to lose it.

I think those Balloon lads did not get all the credit that was due to them. The number of 'doodles' brought down by the balloons is only half the story. I consider they had a job that was no picnic, as the odds were that any buzz-bomb their particular balloon caught would come down on them, and the lads around here had some narrow escapes.

"From the beginning of the arrival of the V1 flying bombs, barrage balloons had been moored at *Valance* and up parallel with Vicarage Hill, all along behind *Breaches* and *The Pheasantry*, at Horley Corner, the length of Pilgrims' Way and along the top of Westerham Hill."

We were more than pleased when Jerry gave it a rest. We certainly needed one and were getting a bit bleary-eyed before the end. In time we said good-bye to the balloons with little regret, although we were very sorry to see some good friends go with them.

Others who had had more than enough of Jerry were Westerham's POWs who arrived home by air from a defeated Germany, where towards the end of their long enforced absence in Poland and Germany, they had witnessed with hope for an early deliverance from prison existence, the massive sorties of our bombers on raids over Europe.

WVS For Civil Defence. Archive material.

Extracts taken from the Chairman's report:

...The Mobile Canteen fed over 100 Civil Defence and NFS personnel when a Nursery School received a direct hit from a flying bomb in this area. During the evacuation of school children in July and again on their return in December, the Mobile Canteen supplied tea and sandwiches to approximately 170 WVS members and evacuees.

Army Mending: During the first six months of the year 614 garments were mended for the Army.

Camouflage Nets: Depots functioned at Westerham, Brasted and Toys Hill until Camouflage Net work ceased in August 1944, by which time over 400 large nets and 2,338 small ones had been completed.

Knitting: Members have worked for the Kent County Comforts Organisation, the Merchant Navy and European Clothing Relief, and in all 270lbs of wool has been knitted into nearly 800 garments.

On July 4th (1944) the WVS co-operated with the Women's Institute in Edenbridge in caring for relatives of children from Weald House Nursery School, when they came for the Mass Funeral. Lunch and tea were provided, and VCP cars were used extensively.

Balloon Barrage Men: In many villages WVS members helped to look after the RAF men manning the Balloon sites, and on their departure the following letter was received expressing...

... "the very deep appreciation of the officers and men for the most welcome assistance which the members of WVS have accorded us during our stay here. I must confess that, when we first arrived some months ago, we wondered what kind of reception we should receive from the local inhabitants, knowing full well that our very presence meant possible loss and suffering for them from the flying bomb menace, but we go away with the feeling that we have not only done a job of work in our line of duty, but, in the doing of it we have acquired a number of new and very excellent friends. One has only to look at the map recently published to realise how much the County of Kent has taken it on the chin and

thereby saved London from worse destruction than it has already suffered, and we should like to pay our tribute to your County, and particularly to this district for the whole-hearted friendship which has been extended to the men of the Balloon Barrage."

Walter (Jumbo) Gammage
"When I was demobbed, former employers were required to find jobs for six months for their pre-war, now ex-service employees. So B. Horton & Sons were bound to take me back. But they had virtually no wood in the yard, depleted by the requirements of the war years and a lack of imported timber from Russia and Norway. So I went up to the new Labour Exchange at *Winterton Court* where they told me that there was really no need for people even to go to Labour Exchanges. There was so much work around that people were getting themselves sorted out. I was early into uniform, so early out and older than many, and I soon found a job."

Hitler was dead, Berlin had fallen to the Russians and in Italy all German forces had surrendered. By 2 May 1945 it was clear that the war in Europe was over.

Announcement by the Board of Trade, 7 May 1945.
Until the end of May you may buy cotton bunting without coupons, as long as it is red, white or blue and does not cost more than 1s3d a quarter yard.

Joan Myhill (née Kimber)
"On VE Day at Charlie Sharp's Garage where my husband Reg worked they had trestle tables up for a celebration lunch sort of thing. I wasn't able to stay long as I had Peter and Pam, small children at home in New Street, but the celebration party probably carried on all day and into the evening. Elizabeth was born in 1940 in the middle of the Battle of Britain. We used to dive down into the cellar every time the siren went. Nurse Ford was really marvellous but she hated the blackout and air raids so much that Reg used to drive her home. He also drove Mr Churchill up to London every so often, as reserve chauffeur to Joe (Frank) Jenner, popping in to collect his 'chauffeur's' jacket for the occasion as it was usually a short-notice call. If there was a diversion because of bomb damage or an unexploded bomb, Mr Churchill who would appear to be totally engrossed behind his newspaper, would react immediately and comment on the change of route between Chartwell and Downing Street."

Beryl Bellingham (née Martin), Joy Edgar (née Herbert) and June Smith (née Jenner)
"On VE Night, a whole crowd of us foregathered at Charlie Sharp's ga-

rage and danced in that huge yard at the back where there once was the old fire station. They used to send up flares for fires and they let one off on VE night. They had set up trestle tables and put on a wonderful spread considering the rationing. It was an unforgettable victory party."

"Did we have Bertie Mombrun, our local master of ceremonies with his gramophone and drum accompaniment? Joan Mombrun (née Fisk) thinks he might just have been demobbed and home from the RAF. And was Jack Cattaway (Charlie Sharp's pre-war Manager at the garage who had joined up in the RAF?) also home again at *Willards Croft*? I just remember that they did wonders with spam and fish-paste sandwiches spread about with a lot of green garnish. And there were jellies too, in primary colours speckled with tinned fruit and decorated with frills of piped imitation cream."

Margaret Tulloch (née Johnson)
"We were all dancing there, my parents too, and somebody had got hold of some army thunder flashes and they were letting them off in amongst the dancers which was getting pretty dangerous. The Gordon Highlanders had their mess in *Squerryes Court* and they might have brought them along. They were like big fire-crackers."

"All the tables were decorated with vases of red, white (Cow Parsley) and blue flowers and we had that wonderful war news from one of those dear broadcasters and war correspondents...was it Bruce Belfrage, Alvar Lidell, John Snagge, Freddie Grisewood, Frank Gillard or Wynford Vaughan Thomas I wonder now?...and then the King's speech at 9.0 over the wireless. I suppose each of us has a different memory of that unforgettable evening."

Don Adams
"On VE day, 8 May 1945, we danced in the corner of the corn field where we had been threshing. Someone in the little row of *Squerryes Park Cottages* where the estate workers lived, produced an old gramophone and some records which we played. With flags tied around the top of the threshing machine we just danced around out in that corn field on the right-hand-corner where the Goodley Stock Road meets the A25. Then the boss came out and told us all to get on with our work: 'it ain't over yet' he kept saying...but we all jolly well knew it was, because we'd heard it on the wireless."

Phil Johnson
"On VE night Dad was one of a gang who got very merry(I'm told) and along with others in Crockham Hill, they celebrated by taking this great stone ball off a pillar at the entrance to the drive of a big house up the hill and let it roll

down through the village." (Could it have come from *Crockham Hill Farm*, or *The Old Farmhouse*? Between them they have three splendid stone balls). "It rumbled right down through the village to rousing cheers, making a noise like a roaring train until it finished up at *The Rushetts* on the way to Edenbridge. There was a tremendous enquiry afterwards to try to find out who was responsible for such a dangerous prank. But Crockham Hill had been well away that VEDay evening and no one person could have been held responsible."

11 May 1945. Westerham Infant School Records.

A short service of Thanksgiving for the ending of the war in Europe was held in the school

"In school the day after VE Day we each got a red apple from Canada."

18 May 1945. Hosey School Records.

All children went to Westerham at 4.0 to hear Mr Winston Churchill speak to the people of the town.

Don Adams
"When VJ Day came along, somehow it wasn't the same...it all fell a bit flat. But on the day that we danced in that corn field, that same evening we had a giant bonfire in Crockham Hill, just where the roads meet opposite the post office and close to The Royal Oak. Everyone brought things to throw on the fire and the firemen were frightened we'd set light to some haystacks nearby. We even made a hole in the road where we burnt all the tarmac out."

Phil Johnson
"I remember a feeling of disappointment to have missed the war. The war never really touched me. Dad was too old to join up and we were all very young. We never lost a relative that I know of though I lost friends during the *Blitz*, bombed out or evacuated. We never underestimated what was going on, but we lived in our own busy world. It all seems very insular, looking back, but never defeatist, ever."

Sadly it was right at the end of the war that much damage was done to *Squerryes Court* when the RASC arrived to be 'de-mobbed.'

John Warde
"They did weapons' training with Bren guns on the lawn and had parades out here in front of the house in the forecourt. There were slit trenches up the

back that we have now filled in, into which my mother always said the troops wearing their tin hats used to disappear whenever the siren went, whereas everyone else just carried on with what they were doing. But as a small child it was the humming sound made by the wind whistling through the metal hawsers of the barrage balloons, and seeing trout fished from our lake and kept swimming around in our baths, that are some of my most poignant wartime memories."

The Rev. Oliver Fielding Clarke
The day peace was declared was a wonderfully sunny day and the little church was packed to overflowing for an impromptu thanksgiving service. It was incredible how, in such a scattered parish, the news of the service got round and the ringing of our solitary bell well beforehand quickly told those who had not heard by word of mouth of our arrangements.

There were, I think, about a dozen men from the village killed in the war, and we very soon had their names inscribed on a board in church, fixed immediately below that which commemorated the fallen of the First World War, and this I dedicated at a special service. Gradually the rest of the young men were demobilized and we soon had enough to raise a football team, which I used to watch play sometimes on a Saturday afternoon.

Eventually we collected enough money to buy a field for permanent use, both for football and cricket and also other sports. This became our principal village war memorial, for I had been against the erection of any costly marble or granite cross or obelisk in the main street. The tablet in church was all that was needed to recall the names of the fallen and it was better to devote the bulk of the money we could get to contribute something which would improve village life for future generations. I am sure this would have pleased those who had given their lives. The Bishop, who had been an Olympic runner as well as getting his 'blue' at Oxford, came down to dedicate the field and its memorial gates as soon as they were ready.

On 18 May 1945, ten days after VE day the Whitsun week-end brought an opportunity to relax, as the people of Westerham prepared to enjoy their first public holiday for six years. Early that Friday morning via Mrs Bill Cosgrove, word had got around that the Prime Minister, on his way home to Chartwell, would be stopping off in Westerham. The news of his coming having travelled ahead of him, Charlie Sharp is credited with having set in train the spontaneous 'Welcome Home' that would take place later that afternoon on the Green.

Beryl Bellingham and Joyce Hoath were cycling home that evening from their Land Army jobs working for farmer Bernard Bush at Crockham Hill's Model Farm, when they found Westerham full of excited crowds.

"Everyone was heading towards the Green so we got on our heavy old Land Army bikes and followed them up there, and just at that moment, there was Mr Churchill getting out of his car...and he shook hands with me and said: 'Well done!'"

Mr and Mrs Churchill were received by members of the Parish Council and given a rousing welcome by as many local residents as could get there - rationed petrol permitting. Westerham's returned Prisoners of War too were welcomed home, publicly and individually, each one in due course to receive from the Parish Council a citation of appreciation for his or her war service. From a farm wagon the Prime Minister shared in the peoples' enthusiasm over victory and was cheered to the echo. The little girl injured by the rocket that had crashed on to Madan Road in March of that year, presented a large bouquet of flowers to Mrs Churchill.

Edythe Samuel (née Curtis)
"I was fetched home from Orpington Hospital where I was still being treated for a shrapnel wound to my right arm. I remember being dressed in a pale mauve party frock which had had the sleeve slit to accommodate my plaster casing. But being something of a tomboy, I didn't really want to be all dressed up and on show, and lifted up on to that farm-wagon platform. I was taken first to *Churchgate* to wait there with that huge bunch of flowers to present to Mrs Churchill. I can't remember what she said to me, but Mr Churchill gave me a kiss. At the time it was all a bit overwhelming, but to-day I can appreciate that kindly kiss.

I have scarcely any memories of the incident itself. I just know that I was out in our garden near the bridge in Madan Road, and of course being a V2, there was no warning and therefore no siren. It didn't knock me out and I remained standing up and tried to walk up the steps but couldn't get into the house because the door had been blown off its hinges and was jammed at an angle.

Then some of the soldiers billeted at *Oak Lodge* who had hurried to the scene, bundled me into a house up the road. They bound up my forearm, which was hanging down with both bones broken, in towels and things. It must have been they who contacted Joe Jenner who took me in his taxi, all on his own, to a first aid post in Dunton Green. He had been at Hosey School with my father, Walter Curtis and of course I knew him.

From there I was transferred to Sevenoaks Hospital and then to Orpington. My mother who had been in the kitchen cooking Sunday lunch didn't even know where I was. Our house was next-door to where poor Mr George Blake was killed instantly in his garden adjoining ours, just a few yards from where I was standing."

"Westerham was decorated with Union Jacks, Maple leaves and Stars and Stripes, and men from the Gordon Highlanders stationed locally, and boys from Westerham's RAF Cadet unit were on parade on the Green. The flag that flew from a staff near St Mary's Church was:

> PRESENTED BY
> 953 BALLOON SQUADRON
> R.A.F. OCTOBER 1944
> THIS FLAGSTAFF WAS USED BY
> THE UNIT WHILST STATIONED IN
> COSTELLS'S MEADOW

But best of all, was the presence of our prisoners of war who had just arrived home and who were all welcomed with heart-warming cheers. It had been six long years since they had left Westerham and later many had been captured in France."

Margot Clark (née Sumner)
"My husband Colin, whom I married on 2 September 1939 and who was amongst the first British troops to be taken prisoner at Dunkirk, returned home with a useless arm, with the first batch of POWs to be repatriated. We met again almost as strangers, at the Grosvenor Hotel at Victoria Station. All we had had was two or three days of life together and five and a half years of wartime separation. We'd been married all those years and done nothing with them. It was a bad and very traumatic start, but we got over it and triumphed in the end, living first at *Millers Mead* in Hosey Hill and then at *White Timbers* at Goodley Stock."

28 May 1945. WPC
Matters discussed were:
The authorisation of expenditure for celebrating the termination of organised hostilities in Europe.
Street lighting.
The requested removal of the static water dam and road blocks from The Green.
The proposed scheme for a Commemoration Fund.
The few vacant allotments, and Lady Pelham's possible desire for her land to be released.

Cr A.F.E. Brunsden asked if the Council would approve of an official letter of welcome being sent to returning members of the Forces.

...Warde land earmarked for use as a Recreation Ground. Major Marnham

179

(of Chartwell Farm) remarked on the hardship that would be felt by Crockham Hill and that he was inclined to object. On being assured that Westerham would support Crockham Hill in a similar scheme, he withdrew his objection.

Major Marnham reported hedges overhanging at Buttle's Steps and over footpaths known as Jacob's Ladder and a path leading to Guildables by Model Farm Crockham Hill. Complaints were voiced about the stagnant water in the Dam.

Life was getting back to normal.

"One of the things I had missed most during those years of blacked-out war, were no lights from windows and not being able to go towards the welcome of a lit and open doorway."

The matters which concerned the WPC in May continued to be discussed throughout the summer until , at the meeting on 3 September 1945, the matter of the dam was resolved when it was suggested, and agreed, that an application be made for Prisoners of War to do the work and charge the cost to the Home Office.

In the event, 28 concrete road blocks set up by the Army to protect Westerham from invading enemy tanks and military vehicles in 1940 were, literally, put out to grass. Having earlier served as a base for the old groundsman's hut, to-day, possibly unrecognized for what they once were, they form a long tubular line against a hedge on King George's Playing Field. And some of the fine Kentish rag-stone recovered from the old fire station in Post Office Square has now been incorporated into the pillars of the entrance gateway to King George's Playing Field.

As thousands of American troops made their way home from Europe via this country, many landed at the Channel ports and eventually headed inland along the A25. Driving through Westerham they dispensed largesse in the form of German Military and *Luftwaffe* badges to the local girls who had turned out to cheer and welcome them, some of whom treasure those war trophies to this day.

At the end of 1945, a committee under the Chairmanship of Mr S.D. Gladstone of *Lewins* was formed to consider the question of a War Memorial to the 11 members of Crockham Hill who lost their lives. An appeal for funds was most generously supported and over £2,200 was subscribed by the people of Crockham Hill. At a public meeting held early in 1946, it was decided that the War Memorial should take the form of a playing field, and a committee under the Chairmanship of Lt. Col. Arthur Mills and represented by all local clubs and associations, was formed to carry out this scheme.

25 March 1946. WPC minutes:

Victory Celebrations:
Ministry of Health (under Section 228(1) Local Government Act 1933) sanctions any reasonable expenses which may be incurred by Councils in connection with any public local Victory Celebrations, in so far as these expenses are charged in accounts subject to audit by a District auditor.

18 February 1946. WPC minutes:

War Memorial:
Cr G.H. Streatfeild mentioned that there was a suggestion to inscribe the names of the fallen on the War Memorial standing in the Churchyard. Cr W.E. Bennett proposed, Cr A.C. Sharp seconded that the Council raise no objection.

15 April 1946. WPC minutes:

Victory Day Celebrations:
Cr P.E. Dicks stated that the clubs and other bodies in the town were waiting to see if the Council were contributing towards the occasion, and gave an outline of the provisional proposals.
Cr C. Dence proposed, Cr H. Farmer seconded that the Council raise £120 by a 1d rate to be divided, £80 for Westerham Ward and £40 for Crockham Hill Ward.

And on this same day, Westerham celebrated its Victory in Europe Day with Joyce Oldfield as Carnival Queen and a Victory Tableau representing America, Russia, France and China. John Warde remembers watching the procession from the Papillons home, *The White Cottage* in the Croydon Road.

"At 11.00 am there was a carnival with fancy dress competitions. Sports on the King George VI Playing Field at 2.30 pm were followed by a baby show, a childrens' tea in the Womens' Institute and an old peoples' tea in St Mary's Hall.

After tea there was a relay race, a tug-of-war final, prizes given, community singing on The Green at 7.30 pm and a carnival dance at St Mary's Hall from 8 pm to midnight. Altogether a day to remember, in aid of the War Com-

On 8 June 1946 all school-age children were given an illuminated citation signed by H.M. King George VI.

8th June, 1946

To-day, as we celebrate victory, I send this personal message to you and all other boys and girls at school. For you have shared in the hardships and dangers of a total war and you have shared no less in the triumph of the Allied Nations.

I know you will always feel proud to belong to a country which was capable of such supreme effort; proud, too, of parents and elder brothers and sisters who by their courage, endurance and enterprise brought victory. May these qualities be yours as you grow up and join in the common effort to establish among the nations of the world unity and peace.

George R.I

memoration Fund which was to provide the town with its Memorial Pavilion on the King George V1 Playing Field."

Phil Johnson
"I was working at the Wolfe Garage just after the war when Mr. Churchill was a customer. He had an old pre-war chainsaw which was always breaking down. My father, Fred, was called to Chartwell to fix it, yet again, when they were cutting down an enormous tree. Winston had a gang of German prisoners still working for him whilst, I presume, they were awaiting repatriation. When Dad came back he said: 'You can see who won the war.' The troops, under their commanding officer, were apparently slicing away with a huge crosscut saw whilst Churchill sat back in his wicker chair with his cigar, and watched them. In fact the German prisoners really respected him."

Apart from the graves still cared for by families and friends, there are nine in Westerham Churchyard which are looked after by the Imperial War Graves Commission and the British Legion, one of which is that of a Canadian soldier, and another a Belgian. These last two died during the First World War.

Victory dinner at the King's Arms, Westerham for Home Guard officers and distinguished guests. Men in this photograph include Ned Funnell (seated left), Fred Shergold (centre foreground), Mr Bagnall (standing centre) and Sir Charles Pym (far right) of Foxwold, Brasted, later to become chairman of Kent County Council.

WESTERHAM

Victory Day

WESTERHAM'S VICTORY QUEEN.

MISS JOYCE OLDFIELD.

VICTORY TABLEAU.

Britannia :
Miss Joyce Oldfield.

America :
Miss Joan Eatwell.

Russia :
Miss Pamela Whiting.

China :
Miss Pauline Musaphia.

France :
Miss Audrey Dunn.

CARNIVAL

Judges—
Major and Mrs. J. R. O'B. Warde
Sir Henry Pelham
Mr. and Mrs. L. C. Knight.
Mr. and Mrs. E. M. Powell
Mr. and Mrs. B. W. Robinson
Mr. and Mrs. J. O. Robson.

Chief Marshal : C. Bell

Organising Marshal : P. J. Smart

Entries will be judged at 11 a.m. in the Market Field.

FANCY DRESS.

Entries will be accepted up to 10.45 a.m. on Saturday.

Class 1. Girls under 10.

Class 2. Boys under 10.

Class 3. Girls over 10.

Class 4. Boys over 10.

Class 5. Ladies.

Class 6. Gentlemen.

WESTERHAM 1939 - 1945

Richard Stafford Allen
Charles John Bassett
Robert Ernest Bell
Cecil Graham Boakes
William Boakes
William Ernest Booker
Norman Addison Bramwell
Michael Burtenshaw
John James Chisholme
John Cecil Currie
Leslie James Edge
Frederick Ian Haslett
Charles Victor Hobbis
William Alfred Hobbis
John Hollingworth

Reginald Martin
Victor Allen Moore
Albert Nicholas
John Allen Nicholas
Alfred George Stanley
Robert Stone
Norman Roland Streatfeild
James Champion Streatfeild
Arnold Taylor
Frank Townsend Taylor
Frederick Taylor
Ernest Terry
George Albert Turnage
Sidney Watts
Albert Bernard Webster

Westerham and Crockham Hill War Memorials

THIS FIELD IS DEDICATED TO THOSE WHO LOST THEIR LIVES IN WAR 1939-1945 GIVEN BY THE PEOPLE OF CROCKHAM HILL

DICK BAGGS
CECIL BARNES
CHARLES BRYANT
RICHARD HOOD
JOHN LYNCH
HUBERT MALCOMSON

D. VAN OOSTERWYK BRUYN
ERNEST TERRY
SOLOMON WAGHORN
ROBIN WRIGHT
TOM WRIGHT

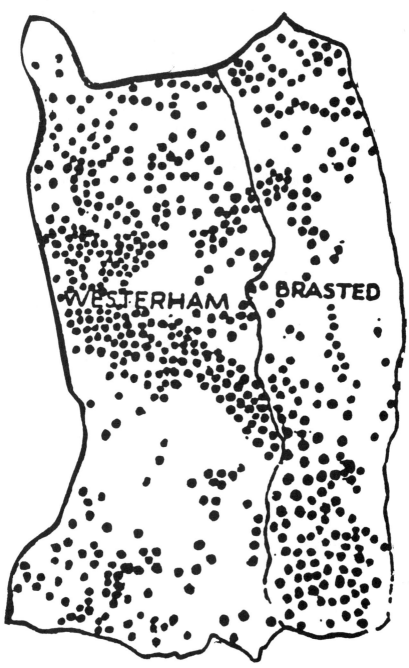

Black dots show the high explosives which fell in Westerham and Brasted — two of the most heavily bombed areas in Kent.

BIBLIOGRAPHY

The Second World War. Vol. IV. The Hinge of Fate. Winston Churchill. Cassell. 1951

A Churchill Family Album Mary Soames. Allen Lane. 1982

Churchill and Chartwell. Robin Fedden. A National Trust Guide. Printed by The Westerham Press. Pergamon Press. 1968

Biggin on the Bump. Bob Ogley. Froglets Publications. 1990

Doodlebugs and Rockets. Bob Ogley. Froglets Publications 1992

Scramble. Norman Gelb. Michael Joseph. 1986

Front Line County. Andrew Rootes. Robert Hale. 1980

The Day War Broke Out. Compiled and Edited by Kevin Black. 1989

Churchill -Townsman of Westerham. Percy C. Reid. Regency International Publications. 1969

Leigh in the War 1939-1945. Compiled and Edited by Morgen Witzel. Leigh & District Historical Society. Occasional Paper Number Two. 1993

Aspects of Edenbridge. Issue Number 10. Edenbridge in WWII. Editor Wynne M. Griffiths. 1994

Westerham Valley Railway. Locomotion Papers Number Seventy-Two. David Gould. The Oakwood Press. 1974.

The Way We Lived Then. Norman Longmate. Hutchinson. 1971

Life in Wartime Britain. E.R. Chamberlin. B.T. Batsford. 1972

The Rector's Book of Limpsfield. Compiled by Dermott W. Thompson. 1949. Entries by the Rev. Charles Steer

Unfinished Conflict. An autobiography by the Rev. Oliver Fielding Clarke. The Citadel Press. 1970

Wing Leader. Group Captain J.E. Johnson, D.S.O. D.F.C. Chatto & Windus. 1956

The First Hundred Years of the Woolwich Equitable Building Society by Colin Brooks. Privately printed. London. 1947

ILLUSTRATIONS

A number of maps, photographs, posters and other illustrations have been used in this book thanks to the following:

Front cover: Children with gas masks (The Rural History Centre, University of Reading).

Front and Rear Endpaper: Ordnance Survey maps of 1936 (HMSO).

Back cover: Winston Churchill presenting long service awards to the special constables who guarded Chartwell during the war (Mr Roland Shergold).

Page 2: Pitts Cottage in 1937 (Helen Long)

Pages 8 & 9: Westerham just at peace 1939: (The Times Newspaper)

P 16: Flight Lieutenant Peter Brothers of 32 Squadron, Biggin Hill with his fiancée and future mother-in-law. (Air Commodore Peter Brothers)

P 21: Tom Gorick with Gordon Cox (Val Doone: This Other Eden)

P 30: Poster (Sevenoaks Library)

Ps 34 & 35: Westerham Home Guard in 1940 (Roland Shergold)

P 47: Bombs at Biggin Hill 1940 (Biggin Hill collection: Bob Ogley)

P 51: Poster (Sevenoaks Library)

P 52: Home Guard veterans at Chartwell (Val Doone: This Other Eden)

P 54: Evacuated children at Crockham Hill (Val Doone: This Other Eden)

P 67: Poster (Sevenoaks Library)

P 68: Poster (Sevenoaks Library)

P 71: Static water tank on Westerham Green (Mrs Cosgrove)

P 73: Signposts removed during invasion fears (Val Doone: This Other Eden)

P 79: Air-raid shelter at Crockham Hill (Val Doone: This Other Eden)

P 85: The Westerham Flyer

P 87: Dance night at Crockham Hill (Val Doone: This Other Eden)

P 97: Bill Cosgrove's sweet shop on Westerham Green (Mrs Cosgrove)

P 108: VAD Nurses (Val Doone: This Other Eden)

Ps 112 & 113: 1914-18 war canons on Westerham Green (Helen Long)

P 119: Churchyard railings (Helen Long)

P 140: Checking identity papers at village barrier (Val Doone: This Other Eden)

P 150: Weald House, Crockham Hill (Bob Ogley)

P 151: Weald House tragedy (Bob Ogley)

Ps 156 & 157: Moorhouse buildings showing the NAAFI (Redlands PLC)

P 162: Flying bomb brought down by barrage balloon (Biggin Hill collection: Bob Ogley)

P 164: Black Eagle beer for the troops

P 166-168: Madan Road rocket (Kent Messenger)

P 182: Victory citation (Mrs Anna Milford)

P 183: Victory dinner at King's Arms, Westerham (Roland Shergold)

P 190: Helen and Aidan Long (Fern Flynn)

Contributors

Adams Don
Allen Kim
Appelt John
Atterbury Rowley
Bailey Ronald
Bell Mons
Bellingham Richard & Beryl
(née Howard)
Bennett Charles
Brayne Richard
Brill Antony
Brothers Air Commodore Peter
Brown George
Brown Leslie (Brownie)
Brydon Rosamund (née James)
Calvocoressi Ion
Capadose Monica (née Bramwell)
Castle John
Charman Ethel (Diamond)
(née Allen)
Churchill School Records
Clemans Philip
Cobley Sally (née Robertshaw)
Collins George.
Combley Robert
Cosgrove Mollie
Couldrey Mollie (née Parker)
Cowell Audrey (née Ricketts)
Cull Fred
Daigle Doris (née Westwood)
Davison Malcolm
(Archivist/Editor Redland PLC)
Darby Olive (née Hazel)
Downs Donald
Eager George
Edgar Gordon & Joy (née Herbert)
Evans Dorothy
(Westerham Parish Council,
Russell House)
Finch Peter
Fleet Margaret
Ernie Fleet.
Fuller Peter
Furst Czeslaw and Joyce (née Cole)
Gammage, Walter (Jumbo)
Gladstone Felicity
Goodwin Alfred & Ruth (née Bedwell)
Gorick Pat (née Penny)
Hankey Helen (née Cassavetti)
Hay Jean
Hayden Phyllis (née Gibbs)
Hewett Beryl (née Furlong)
Hill David (Ranger for East Surrey)

Hoath Geoffrey
Ivey Ted & Gladys (née Whitmore)
Johnson Phil
Kallend Anthony
Kenward Mary (née Petty)
Kindon Geoff & Pat
Knight John
Lee Joy (née Sutherland)
Leworthy Esmé
Lyle Colin
Matthews Alan
McBride Freda (née Wright)
McCosh Fred
Moffatt Ivory
Mombrun Joan (née Fisk)
Myhill Joan (née Kimber)
Nash Graham & Sheila (née Mears)
Ogley Bob
Parker Donald
Peake Edna
Pointon Betty (née Boniface and later Hobbis)
Reynolds Kev
Richards Gladys (née Moore)
Robbins Fiona (KCC Library, Westerham)
Samuel Edythe (née Curtis)
Shergold Roland
Shypitka Peter
Smith June (née Jenner)
Soames Mary (née Churchill)
Steven Peter
Steven Bob
Swarbrick Frederick
Sworder Eileen (née Hay)
Tamplin Anne (née Friend)
Taylor Daisy (née Fuller)
Taylor Malcolm
Thomas Bill
Thomson Marjorie (née Johnson)
Thorneycroft Bert & Joan (née Lelliott)
Tidy May (née Taylor)
Tulloch Peggy (née Johnson)
Turner Ted and Olive (née English)
Warde John O'Brien
Waterhouse 'Len'
Webb Margaret (St Mary the Virgin, Westerham)
Wells Neville
Whittaker-Browne Rosemary
Wilkinson Peggy (Croft Hall School Records)
Williams Sonia (née Mavrogordato)
Wilson Jean (née Knight)
Winder Anthony & Rosamund (née Tyser)
Withers Beryl
Wood Bob
Wood Gwenda
Wybourne Pat (née Bellingham)

Helen and Aidan Long at home in Brasted

About the author

Helen Long (née Vlasto) was born in London in 1920 and educated in London and Hertfordshire. Her father, a Greek, was educated in Paris and Winchester and practiced as a consultant ear, nose and throat surgeon in Wimpole Street. Her mother, although Scottish, was born in the United States.

In 1939 Helen was a "débutante", presented at Court in the spring. Later that year she joined a British Red Cross Society detachment in London and was then assigned to Lambeth Infirmary. The war, however, made allowances for no-one

and Helen volunteered to nurse as a mobile V.A.D. (Voluntary Aid Detachment).

Her experiences were full and varied. She was one of a small detachment of women aboard the troopship Highland Monarch and worked in a naval hospital at Portsmouth where she and her colleagues lovingly nursed the wounded back from a living hell.

In 1946 Helen married Doctor Aidan Long who had served as a Surgeon Lieutenant during the war. Dr Long went into general practice, moving to Westerham in 1946 where he practised for 39 years.

Today they live in Brasted.

KENT AT WAR £10.99 (paperback) £16.99 (hardback)
The Unconquered County by Bob Ogley

This illustrated history of the second world war relives the drama, the heroism and the horrors as they unfolded in Kent — a county in which many people were nearer to occupied Europe than they were to their own capital city. All the great events are here: mobilisation, the evacuation, the phoney war, Dunkirk, the Battle of Britain, the Blitz, the fighter sweeps from Kent airfields, D-Day, the flying bombs and rockets and VE Day in May 1945. This is not just a story of countless fighting men and women but of the ordinary people of the front-line county, from the misery of ration queues and austerity clothing to the delights of Vera Lynn and the flicks. Most of the photographs come from the archives of the Kent Messenger and they cannot fail to stir powerful emotions as they bring back memories of the most dramatic years in the county's history.

Other books from Froglets Publications

In The Wake of The Hurricane
(National Edition Hardback)
ISBN 0 9513019 4 2....................................£9.95

Surrey in The Hurricane
ISBN 0 9513019 2 6....................................£7.50

London's Hurricane
(Paperback) ISBN 0 9513019 3 4.................£4.95
(Hardback) ISBN 0 9513019 8 5.................£7.95

Eye on The Hurricane
Eastern Counties
(Paperback) ISBN 0 9513019 6 9.................£7.95
(Hardback) ISBN 0 9513019 7 7...............£11.95

Biggin On The Bump by Bob Ogley
The story of the most famous fighter station.
(Paperback)ISBN 1 872337 05 8.................£9.99
(Hardback)ISBN 1 872337 10 4 ....£16.95

The Surrey Weather Book
Published by Frosted Earth
ISBN 0 9516710 1 4....................................£7.50

The Sussex Weather Book
ISBN 1 872337 30 9.......................................£9.95

The Kent Weather Book
ISBN 1 872337 35 X.......................................£9.95

The Norfolk and Suffolk Weather Book
(Paperback) ISBN 1 872337 99 6.....................£9.95
(Hardback) ISBN 1 872337 98 8...................£16.95

The Essex Weather Book
ISBN 1 872337 66 X.....................................£9.95

The Hampshire and Isle of Wight Weather Book
ISBN 1 872337 20 1.......................................£9.95

Doodlebugs and Rockets by Bob Ogley
(Hardback) ISBN 1 872337 22 8...................£16.95
(Paperback) ISBN 1 872337 21 X...................£9.95

Flying Bombs over England by H.E. Bates
(Paperback) ISBN 1 872337 18 X.................£10.99
(Hardback) ISBN 1 872337 04 X.................£16.99

King Oak by Ron Denney
(Children's story of the Seven Oaks)
ISBN 1 872337 00 7.......................................£6.95

Froglets Publications, Brasted Chart, Westerham, Kent TN16 ILY

WESTERHAM

Reproduced from the 1936 Ordnance Survey map